YOU CAN HAVE
a new
BEGINNING

BOOKS BY MORRIS CERULLO

How to Pray

AVAILABLE FROM DESTINY IMAGE PUBLISHERS

YOU CAN HAVE
a new
BEGINNING

MORRIS
CERULLO

DESTINY IMAGE® PUBLISHERS, INC.
P.O. Box 310, Shippensburg, PA 17257-0310

"Speaking to the Purposes of God for This Generation and for the Generations to Come."

This book and all other Destiny Image, Revival Press, MercyPlace, Fresh Bread, Destiny Image Fiction, and Treasure House books are available at Christian bookstores and distributors worldwide.

For a U.S. bookstore nearest you, call 1-800-722-6774.
For more information on foreign distributors, call 717-532-3040.
Reach us on the Internet: www.destinyimage.com.

ISBN 10: 0-7684-3196-4
ISBN 13: 978-0-7684-3196-4

For Worldwide Distribution, Printed in the U.S.A.

1 2 3 4 5 6 7 8 9 10 11 / 14 13 12 11 10 09

TABLE OF CONTENTS

INTRODUCTION

This book was not designed to disseminate information. It was written to present a biblical revelation and the application for that revelation. The thesis of this book is simple—yet, profound—if you will only receive it, and act upon it. The message is: You can have a new beginning.

This book does not advocate "turning over a new leaf" or making resolutions at the beginning of a new year. It is not about rehabilitation or therapy to rehash your past or help you to deal with it. Your future is not determined by your past. You may have had a rough start in life, but it does not have to determine your final destiny.

In a time when the very foundations of society and the economy are being shaken, the message of this book is good news. It is based upon the authority of the Word of God, which declares that you can have a new beginning in every area of your life:

> *Therefore if any man be in Christ, he is a new creature: old things are passed away; behold, all things are become new* (2 Corinthians 5:17).

All things become new in Christ. They are not patched up, not rehabilitated, but **new!**

The psalmist declared: *"He restoreth my soul…"* (Ps. 23:3). God uses the original plan—where you were created in His image and glory—to restore you. We are not talking about renovation, rehabilitation, or reformation. We are talking about a true change, from the inside out:

> *Don't become so well-adjusted to your culture that you fit into it without even thinking. Instead, fix your attention on God. You'll be changed from the inside out. Readily recognize*

7

what He wants from you, and quickly respond to it. Unlike the culture around you, always dragging you down to its level of immaturity, God brings the best out of you, develops well-formed maturity in you (Romans 12:2 TM).

You can have a new beginning, despite the fact that:

1. You may have been told that you have an incurable illness. Doctors may have said that there is no hope or no medical recourse for your condition.

2. Your marriage may be in shambles.

3. Your heart may be broken by a wayward son or daughter or an unsaved mate or family member.

4. You may be suffering financial difficulties.

5. You may be battling the effects of emotional or physical abuse.

6. You may be reading this book in prison, serving a life sentence (without the possibility of parole), or sitting on death row. You may think it is too late to begin again or that you have no hope for a new future.

Jesus declared:

The thief cometh not, but for to steal, and to kill, and to destroy: I am come that they might have life, and that they might have it more abundantly (John 10:10).

The enemy—satan—comes to steal, kill, and destroy all that is good in your life. He attacks your relationships, your finances, your health, and your ministry. Jesus declares: *"...I am come that* [you] *might have life...more abundantly"* (John 10:10).

The life of which Jesus spoke is not only eternal life, of which you can be assured by repenting of your sins and accepting Christ as your Savior. Jesus wants you to also have abundant life right now, right where you are, right in this sinful world in which you live, in the midst of your difficult circumstances. He wants you to have a new beginning.

Repeatedly in His Word, God confirms through examples, promises, and declarations that you can have a new beginning. The Word also states that there are two parts to every promise of God: the promise itself and its fulfillment through obedience.

As the steps to a new beginning are presented in this book, you must act on them to make them a reality in your life. You will never have a future as long as you are living in the past. You got to where you are today by doing what you did. If you want things to change, then you must do something differently.

Apostle Paul declared:

> *Brethren, I count not myself to have apprehended: but this one thing I do, forgetting those things which are behind, and reaching forth unto those things which are before, I press toward the mark for the prize of the high calling of God in Christ Jesus* (Philippians 3:13-14).

Don't keep looking back to the past with regret, guilt, or shame. You cannot change the past. Ask God to forgive your past and heal the negative memories. Then look to the future, and ask Him what's next. God said:

> *Behold, I will do a new thing; now it shall spring forth; shall ye not know it? I will even make a way in the wilderness, and rivers in the desert* (Isaiah 43:19).

The question is, are you ready to receive the new thing? Don't settle for your present spiritual level. Don't remain in your comfort zone. Enlarge your vision to encompass a great new beginning!

Enlarge the place of thy tent, and let them stretch forth the curtains of thine habitations: spare not, lengthen thy cords, and strengthen thy stakes; For thou shalt break forth on the right hand and on the left; and thy seed shall inherit the Gentiles [nations], and make the desolate cities to be inhabited. Fear not; for thou shalt not be ashamed: neither be thou confounded; for thou shalt not be put to shame: for thou shalt forget the shame of thy youth... (Isaiah 54:2-4).

God wants you to enlarge your spiritual vision and prepare to receive a new beginning. Your present thinking isn't big enough. Take the limits off God and yourself, and you will break forth into new life on the right hand and on the left. You will be blessed with a new beginning so that you can be a blessing to others.

As you begin this book, stop for a moment, and pray. Commit your past (including all of its associated suffering, abuses, sin, guilt, fear, and shame) to Him. Draw a concluding line on your past right now. By an act of your will, prepare to step into a new future.

As you begin this journey to your new life, you can rest assured that no matter what your circumstances may be (you may be addicted, abused, divorced, abandoned, incarcerated, backslidden, or poverty-stricken), you can begin again.

Judges 3:31 briefly mentions a man named Shamgar. He killed 600 enemy Philistines with an ox goad. He didn't have much going for him in the battle. All he had was a simple ox goad. You may feel that you don't have much going for you to begin again, but take what is in your hand, begin to use it, and watch God do a miracle.

The Bible is filled with stories of those who experienced a new beginning. This book shares their experiences, the principles that enabled them to embrace their new start, and details how you can follow in their footsteps.

Now these things befell them by way of a figure [as an example and warning to us]; they were written to admonish and fit us for right action by good instruction, we in whose days the ages have reached their climax (their consummation and conclud-ing period) (1 Corinthians 10:11 AMP).

It is never too late to begin again and always too early to quit. It's not too late for a new start! You *can* begin again, right now, today! Your best days are still ahead!

CHAPTER 1

YOU CAN HAVE A NEW BEGINNING!

So, do you want a change in your life? Do you want to have a new beginning?

True change does not come through legislation, education, demonstration, or rehabilitation. These are all futile attempts at change that are imposed from the outside. True change comes from the inside, through the power of God's Word being manifested in your life, and through the blood of Jesus Christ:

> *Therefore if any man be in Christ, he is a new creature: old things are passed away; behold, all things are become new. And all things are of God, who hath reconciled us to Himself by Jesus Christ, and hath given to us the ministry of reconciliation; To wit, that God was in Christ, reconciling the world unto Himself, not imputing their trespasses unto them; and hath committed unto us the word of reconciliation* (2 Corinthians 5:17-19).

Reconciliation means "to change from one condition to another" or "a change of one party induced by the action of another."

The biblical message of reconciliation is that because God sent His Son, Jesus Christ, to suffer and die on Calvary, you can be reconciled to God and experience a new beginning in every area of your life. Your soul, spirit, mind, relationships, ministry, finances, and your physical body can all be changed.

When you are reconciled to God, you are dead to the past. Your entire life becomes new:

> *What shall we say, then? Shall we go on sinning so that grace may increase? By no means! We died to sin; how can we live in it any longer? Or don't you know that all of us who were baptized into Christ Jesus were baptized into His death? We were therefore buried with Him through baptism into death in order that, just as Christ was raised from the dead through the glory of the Father, we too may live a new life* (Romans 6:1-4 NIV).

The truth of reconciliation—this change from one condition to another—will be evidenced in every area of your life. New life—that is the essence of the Gospel's message.

EXPERIENCING NEW LIFE

The Bible relates a powerful story of a woman who experienced this new life. This woman was caught in the act of adultery, and the religious leaders were livid. An unruly mob pushed her roughly through the crowd to Jesus.

This woman symbolizes all of those people in the world who are bound by sin and condemned by society. They are without a future and without hope:

> *And the scribes and Pharisees brought unto Him a woman taken in adultery; and when they had set her in the midst, they say unto Him, Master, this woman was taken in adultery, in the very act. Now Moses in the law commanded us, that such should be stoned: but what sayest Thou? This they said, tempting Him, that they might have to accuse him...* (John 8:3-6).

She deserves to die, the scribes and Pharisees declared. The adulterous woman trembled under the accusations of these legalistic leaders. Her reputation was shattered. Her hope was gone. Her very life was hanging in the balance because the penalty for adultery in those days was death by stoning. The angry mob began to pick up stones.

Jesus did not deny this woman's guilt, psychoanalyze her past, or suggest a rehabilitation program. He did not argue with the scribes and Pharisees or start gathering up stones to join them in executing judgment. Jesus didn't say a word. He simply stooped down and began to write on the ground:

> ...But Jesus stooped down, and with His finger wrote on the ground, as though He heard them not. So when they continued asking Him, He lifted up Himself, and said unto them, He that is without sin among you, let him first cast a stone at her. And again He stooped down, and wrote on the ground. And they which heard it, being convicted by their own conscience, went out one by one, beginning at the eldest, even unto the last... (John 8:6-9).

We are not told what Jesus wrote in the sand that day, but we do know that whatever it was, the angry mob quietly departed without another word.

> When Jesus had lifted up Himself, and saw none but the woman, He said unto her, Woman, where are those thine accusers? hath no man condemned thee? She said, No man, Lord. And Jesus said unto her, Neither do I condemn thee; go, and sin no more (John 8:10-11).

ON THE WAY TO A NEW LIFE

When it seemed that all hope was gone, Jesus blotted out this woman's sins, freed her from condemnation, and released her from guilt and shame, which would enable her to embrace a new life.

15

Jesus told the woman, "You are no longer condemned." Do you long to hear these same words? Does your heart cry out for a release from the shame of sin and your past? Are people around you picking up stones and hurling accusations at you because of your failures?

Don't give up. Don't turn away in despair. Don't listen to the negative words of those who declare that you cannot change. Don't let the past dictate your future. God's message to you is just as powerful as the words that Jesus wrote in the sand that day many years ago. His message was written in His blood on the Cross at Calvary. It is a message of reconciliation. It is the message of a new life!

If you do not know Christ as your Savior, then you are condemned to death (like the adulterous woman was) because *"...the wages of sin is death; but the gift of God is eternal life through Jesus Christ our Lord"* (Rom. 6:23).

But the Word declares: *"If we confess our sins, He is faithful and just to forgive us our sins, and to cleanse us from all unrighteousness"* (1 John 1:9). Ask God to forgive your sins and give you a new beginning.

If you are a professing believer, but you feel condemned and rejected like the adulterous woman because of past or present failures, difficulties, or circumstances, the message is the same for you. God wants you to experience a new beginning in every area of your life. He can change every problem, failure, and circumstance in your life. Your future does not have to be like your past.

The angry mob spoke a negative verdict over the woman after she was caught in adultery. She is guilty. She deserves to die! Jesus spoke a different message over the same woman. Are you going to listen to the accusations of those around you, or are you going to listen to the Words that Jesus is speaking over your life?

> *For I know the thoughts that I think toward you, saith the Lord, thoughts of peace, and not of evil, to give you an expected end* (Jeremiah 29:11).

Jesus is speaking words of hope, forgiveness, a new destiny, and a new life. The question is, will you listen to Him?

If you have received Jesus Christ as your Savior, and if *"…the Spirit of him that raised up Jesus from the dead dwell in you, He that raised up Christ from the dead shall also quicken your mortal bodies by His Spirit that dwelleth in you"* (Rom. 8:11). The same Spirit that raised Christ from the dead dwells in you. All you must do is embrace that Spirit of life, and allow Him to operate in your life.

CHAPTER 2

THE PATH TO A NEW BEGINNING

You may be reading this book while on death row or while in prison facing a sentence of life without the possibility of parole. You may have lost your mate and your family due to addictions or wrong choices. Perhaps you have lost everything through great tragedy, and the days ahead of you may seem dark and dismal with no hope for the future.

No matter how deep your sin or how devastated your life, God has a path to a new beginning. This is illustrated through an amazing story of a man named *Gehazi*. Perhaps his name is unfamiliar to you, so let's take some time to review the biblical account of his amazing comeback.

Read Second Kings chapter 5 before continuing. The chapter records the story of a man named *Naaman*. Naaman was the captain of the host of the king of Syria. The Bible records that he was a great man, but he was stricken with the terrible disease, leprosy. Through the efforts of a young captive Israeli maid, Naaman learned about the miracles being done by the prophet of God, Elisha.

In hopes of a miracle to heal his leprosy, Naaman traveled to Elisha's dwelling and took along gifts of silver, gold, and several changes of clothing to present to the prophet.

So Naaman came with his horses and with his chariot, and stood at the door of the house of Elisha. And Elisha sent a messenger unto him, saying, Go and wash in the Jordan seven times, and thy flesh shall come again to thee, and thou shalt be clean.

But Naaman was wroth, and went away, and said, Behold, I thought, He will surely come out to me, and stand, and call on the name of the Lord his God, and strike his hand over the place, and recover the leper. Are not Abana and Pharpar, rivers of Damascus, better than all the waters of Israel? may I not wash in them, and be clean? So he turned and went away in a rage. And his servants came near, and spake unto him, and said, My father, if the prophet had bid thee do some great thing, wouldest thou not have done it? how much rather then, when he saith to thee, Wash, and be clean? Then went he down, and dipped himself seven times in Jordan, according to the saying of the man of God: and his flesh came again like unto the flesh of a little child, and he was clean (2 Kings 5:9-14).

When Naaman returned to the prophet Elisha, he told him: "...*Behold, now I know that there is no God in all earth, but in Israel: now therefore, I pray thee, take a blessing of thy servant*" (2 Kings 5:15). Elisha refused the gifts and sent Naaman on his way to a new life.

Gehazi, Elisha's servant, said to himself: "...*Behold, my master hath spared Naaman this Syrian, in not receiving at his hands that which he brought: but, as the Lord liveth, I will run after him, and take somewhat of him*" (2 Kings 5:20). So Gehazi raced after Naaman and told him that Elisha had reconsidered and decided that he wanted the silver and changes of garments. (Read Second Kings 5:22.)

When Gehazi returned to Elisha's dwelling and stood before his master:

...Elisha said unto him, Whence comest thou, Gehazi? And he said, Thy servant went no whither. And he said unto him, Went not mine heart with thee, when the man turned again

*from his chariot to meet thee? Is it a time to receive money,
and to receive garments, and oliveyards, and vineyards, and
sheep, and oxen, and menservants, and maidservants? The
leprosy therefore of Naaman shall cleave unto thee, and unto
thy seed for ever. And he went out from his presence a leper as
white as snow* (2 Kings 5:25-27).

This was a tragic ending to a promising future. Gehazi served Elisha,
even as Elisha had served Elijah. Perhaps Gehazi would have become a
prophet, following in Elisha's steps, but due to his greed, his future was
aborted. The deadly disease of leprosy descended upon him and would be
passed down to his seed.

Leprosy was one of the worst diseases of Bible times because there was no
cure for it. Since it was contagious, lepers were separated from society. It was
a debilitating disease that destructively ate away a person's flesh. Eventually,
it resulted in death. Leprosy is used as a symbol of sin in the Bible, because
sin is contagious, debilitating, and destructively eats away your life. Left
untreated, sin results in death.

IN THE PRESENCE OF THE KING

You might think that after contracting leprosy, Gehazi would fade from
the pages of Scripture, but in Second Kings chapter 6, we find him in an
unusual place. He is in the presence of the king:

*And the king talked with Gehazi the servant of the man of
God, saying, Tell me, I pray thee, all the great things that
Elisha hath done. And it came to pass, as he was telling the
king how he had restored a dead body to life, that, behold,
the woman, whose son he had restored to life, cried to the
king for her house and for her land. And Gehazi said, My
Lord, O king, this is the woman, and this is her son, whom
Elisha restored to life. And when the king asked the woman,
she told him. So the king appointed unto her a certain*

*officer, saying, Restore all that was hers, and all the fruits of
the field since the day that she left the land, even until now*
(2 Kings 8:4-6).

What was Gehazi doing in the king's throne room? What was he doing
in the king's employ? Lepers were outcasts of society. People with leprosy
didn't serve in the throne room of the king. Yet, we find Gehazi in the presence of the king.

The answer is found by examining the events that transpired between
Second Kings chapter 5 and Second Kings chapter 8. In Second Kings chapter
7, the prophet Elisha pronounced judgment on the people living in the city of
Samaria because of their unconfessed sin. Samaria came under the siege of its
enemy, Syria. Supplies were cut off, and a famine resulted in the city.

Outside the city gates sat four leprous men. They eventually came to a
realization:

*…Why sit we here until we die? If we say, We will enter into
the city, then the famine is in the city, and we shall die there:
and if we sit still here, we die also. Now therefore come, and let
us fall unto the host of the Syrians: if they save us alive, we shall
live; and if they kill us, we shall but die* (2 Kings 7:3-4).

These men realized that to remain where they were was certain death.
To go into Samaria was death also, as there was a great famine in the city. So,
they made a decision. They rose up in the twilight and went into the camp
of the Syrians, but to their surprise, the camp was deserted. God had caused
the Syrians to hear a noise that sounded like chariots and horses, and they
fled, leaving their belongings behind. (Read Second Kings 7:5-7.)

*And when these lepers came to the uttermost part of the camp,
they went into one tent, and did eat and drink, and carried
thence silver, and gold, and raiment, and went and hid it; and
came again, and entered into another tent, and carried thence
also, and went and hid it. Then they said one to another, We*

do not well: this day is a day of good tidings, and we hold our peace: if we tarry till the morning light, some mischief will come upon us: now therefore come, that we may go and tell the king's household (2 Kings 7:8-9).

The lepers came to the city and delivered the good news. At first, the king thought that it might be a trick and they were part of an ambush, so he sent some men to check out the camp. They returned with the report that the camp was abandoned. The hungry people descended and took the spoils of food, water, gold, silver, and garments.

Orthodox Jewish rabbis believe that the lepers who were sitting outside the gate were Gehazi and his three sons. When they made the decision to go into the abandoned camp, the Bible says that one said to the others: "*... We do not well...*" (2 Kings 7:9). It is believed that this was Gehazi speaking. Remember that his original sin had involved gold, silver, and changes of garments. As he saw these treasures again, free for the taking, he remembered what happened to him the last time and made a decision that would change his destiny. This time, he did it right.

WHY SIT THERE AND DIE?

Gehazi was stricken with leprosy, and the same judgment passed on to his sons. One day—sick, starving, devastated, and near death—he declared, "Why sit we here until we die?" Like Gehazi, if you are to embrace a new life, then you must get up from the circumstances in which you find yourself, and begin to move toward your destiny.

The Bible says the lepers rose up in twilight. Twilight is the darkest time of the day. In this, the darkest time of your life, you must determine to rise up and begin to move toward your destiny. The Bible also says that the Syrians had heard the sound of a great host at twilight and fled. When these lepers rose up in their weakness, God manifested Himself, and the enemy fled.

When Gehazi saw the Syrian treasures, it probably reminded him of his great sin involving the garments and silver that he had wrongfully taken from Naaman. He determined not to fail that test again! He gathered the other lepers, and they went to the city to share the good news. As in the New Testament pattern, as they went, they were healed.

No one thought a leper could be changed. People may not believe that you can change. You may not think you can change. Regardless of your sin, regardless of the curses passed down by your parents, you can experience a new start.

In the Book of Joel, God declared about errant Israel:

> *That which the palmerworm hath left hath the locust eaten; and that which the locust hath left hath the cankerworm eaten; and that which the cankerworm hath left hath the caterpiller eaten* (Joel 1:4).

These pests were sent by God because of sin, but Israel would be restored through repentance:

> *And I will restore to you the years that the locust hath eaten, the cankerworm, and the caterpillar, and the palmerworm, my great army which I sent among you. And ye shall eat in plenty, and be satisfied, and praise the name of the Lord your God, that hath dealt wondrously with you: and My people shall never be ashamed* (Joel 2:25-26).

God will restore the effects of sin and liberate you from sexual bondage, drugs, alcohol, and anything else that enslaves you. He will restore all of your wasted years. You may have been deeply scarred by the sin, the leprosy of this world. You may have the curses of addictions or sexual impurity operating in your life. You may have committed the vilest sin and think that all hope is gone, but as illustrated by the story of Gehazi, you can be restored. In Second Kings chapter 8, we find the formerly leprous Gehazi serving as the king's right-hand man, an example of God's mercy that shares the message of His saving and delivering power.

Don't sit there and die. Get up, and begin to move toward your new life.

CHAPTER 3

WINNING THE BATTLE
FOR YOUR MIND

Perhaps the greatest battle that you will have in embracing this new life will occur in your mind. For certain, the woman who was caught in adultery had a mental battle when she began her new life. Satan surely reminded her of her past and tried to make her think that she would be unable to go her way and to sin no more. Gehazi must have battled with the negative ramifications of his time as a leper and the sin and shame that brought this terrible judgment on him and his family.

One of the major spiritual battlefields is your mind. That is where satan brings up accusations of your past, peddles his deceiving lies, and aborts your hope for a new future. If you are to have a new beginning, you must—through the power of Jesus Christ—take control of your mind. True change comes from the inside out. Your mind must be changed.

Because spiritual change is just that, spiritual, it must be understood with a spiritual mind. In our natural, sinful state, we cannot understand spiritual things:

> But the natural man receiveth not the things of the Spirit of God: for they are foolishness unto him; neither can he know them, because they are spiritually discerned (1 Corinthians 2:14).

Ask God to give you a spiritual mind that can receive the words of new life He will speak to you through the pages of this book.

KEY STRATEGIES OF SATAN

There are six major strategies that satan will use to try to abort your new beginning.

1. *Discouragement*

Discouragement means to be "without courage." Satan wants to discourage you because if you are "without courage," you will not be able to rise up and embrace the new life God wants to give you. When satan tries to bring discouragement, claim this verse:

> *Have not I commanded thee? Be strong and of a good courage;*
> *be not afraid, neither be thou dismayed: for the Lord thy God*
> *is with thee whithersoever thou goest* (Joshua 1:9).

Reword this verse to make it personal. Declare that *God has commanded me to be strong and of a good courage; to not be afraid or dismayed: The Lord my God is with me wherever I go!*

2. *Depression*

Satan also causes depression, the hopeless feeling that things cannot and will not change. To be depressed is to be downcast, sad, discouraged, or in low spirit. It includes feelings of despair, despondency, and dejection. Depression can lead to suicidal thoughts and actual suicide because of the hopeless feelings that produce uncontrollable mental grief, sorrow, heartache, and crying.

Sometimes satan uses your circumstances to lead to depression. A great loss or fear of loss, suppressed anger, a low self-concept, unfulfilled expectations, and a negative attitude can all cause depression. Sometimes depression results from the negative attitudes of those around you through whom satan works. In Deuteronomy 1:28 God's people admitted: *"...our brethren have discouraged our hearts."*

Do not let depression rule you. When you feel its tentacles wrapping around your soul, bind it in the name of Jesus and begin to praise and worship God. Depression cannot remain where praise and worship rule. Declare the words of the psalmist David:

> *I waited patiently for the Lord; and He inclined unto me, and heard my cry. He brought me up also out of an horrible pit, out of the miry clay, and set my feet upon a rock, and established my goings. And He hath put a new song in my mouth, even praise unto our God: many shall see it, and fear, and shall trust in the Lord* (Psalm 40:1-3).

3. Wrong Attitudes and Emotions

Satan inserts into your mind fiery darts of envy, jealousy, suspicion, unforgiveness, distrust, anger, hatred, intolerance, prejudice, impatience, judgment, criticism, covetousness, and selfishness. He also causes wrong attitudes of greed, discontent, pride, vanity, ego, and self-righteousness. Wrong attitudes lead to wrong emotions and both stem from your thoughts.

Left unresolved, these attitudes and emotions will abort your new beginning. Take time each day to examine your heart and ask forgiveness if you have allowed these attitudes and emotions into your life.

4. Rebellion

Rebellion is willful disobedience against God's authority. Rebellion was the original sin of satan as his five statements of "I will" demonstrate in Isaiah 14:12-14. The "I will" spirit is a way to recognize the operation of satan through rebellion.

As long as you are directing your own way and rebelling against God, you will never have a new beginning. Ask God to reveal any rebellion, repent of it, and ask Him to take full control of your life.

5. Accusation and Condemnation

Satan is called the accuser of the brethren (see Rev. 12:10). He causes feelings of shame, unworthiness, and embarrassment.

Accusation by the enemy is not the same as conviction by the Holy Spirit. A good way to tell the difference between the conviction of the Holy Spirit and the condemnation of satan is to remember that satan always generalizes. For example, satan speaks into your mind thoughts like these: *You are no good. You can never live a Christian life. God couldn't love you because you are too great of a sinner.* By contrast, when the Holy Spirit is convicting you, it is specific. For example, He might bring to your attention that you responded to someone in anger and should seek forgiveness.

When satan brings condemnation, use this verse:

> *There is therefore now no condemnation to them which are in Christ Jesus, who walk not after the flesh, but after the Spirit* (Romans 8:1).

6. Fear

Fear can prevent you from embracing your new life, just as it prevented Israel from entering their Promised Land. You fear change and you also fear that things cannot change.

Fear could have kept Gideon and his entire nation from a new beginning. When the angel appeared to Gideon with a directive from God to deliver His people, he was hiding from the enemy:

> *And there came an angel of the Lord, and sat under an oak which was in Ophrah, that pertained unto Joash the Abiezrite: and his son Gideon threshed wheat by the winepress, to hide it from the Midianites. And the angel of the Lord appeared unto him, and said unto him, The Lord is with thee, thou mighty man of valour. And Gideon said unto him, Oh my Lord, if the Lord be with us, why then is all this befallen us? and where be all His miracles which our fathers told us of, saying, Did not the Lord bring us up from Egypt? but now the Lord hath forsaken us, and delivered us into the hands of the Midianites* (Judges 6:11-13).

Here was a man so paralyzed by fear that he was hiding from the enemy, yet the angel addresses him as a mighty man of valor.

> *And the Lord looked upon him, and said, Go in this thy might, and thou shalt save Israel from the hand of the Midianites: have not I sent thee? And he said unto Him, Oh my Lord, wherewith shall I save Israel? behold, my family is poor in Manasseh, and I am the least in my father's house. And the Lord said unto him, Surely I will be with thee, and thou shalt smite the Midianites as one man* (Judges 6:14-16).

Despite all his excuses and fears, Gideon was seen by God as a mighty man of valor. You need to start seeing yourself as God sees you. Start agreeing with God that you are a mighty spiritual warrior. Stop running from the enemy, fearing, and expecting to fail.

When satan comes with tormenting feelings of fear, use these Scriptures:

> *There is no fear in love; but perfect love casteth out fear; because fear hath torment. He that feareth is not made perfect in love* (1 John 4:18).

> *For God hath not given us the spirit of fear; but of power, and of love, and of a sound mind* (2 Timothy 1:7).

SPIRITUAL COUNTER-STRATEGIES

There is no doubt that the greatest hindrance to your new beginning is your mind. Here are seven tremendous counter-strategies God has given for overcoming mental attacks of satan intended to abort your new life.

1. Let the Holy Spirit Search Your Mind

Ask God to search your mind and reveal to you any wrong attitudes, motives, and thoughts that would hinder your new beginning. Pray this prayer:

Search me, O God, and know my heart; try me, and know my
thoughts: And see if there be any wicked way in me, and lead
me in the way everlasting (Psalm 139:23-24).

As the Holy Spirit reveals things to you, act on the revelation. Ask
forgiveness for wrong thoughts and use the Word of God to develop new
thought patterns that will open your spirit to a new beginning.

2. Use Your Spiritual Armor

Three pieces of spiritual armor defend you from attacks in the mind.
These are listed in Ephesians 6:16-17.

The first is the helmet of the hope of salvation. A helmet is worn on the
head and implies protection to the mind. The believer who has the helmet
of salvation in place understands God is working out His eternal purpose of
salvation. He is not disturbed by the attacks of the enemy. He has hope not
only for the present, but for the future.

The second piece of spiritual armor for mental protection is the shield
of faith. The word *faith* not only refers to the basic truths of the Gospel, but
also to your confidence in God. Faith gives you the ability to believe that you
can receive a new beginning.

The third piece of spiritual armor is the girdle of truth (see Eph. 6:14).
The truth of God's Word defeats false accusations of the enemy and confirms
God's promises to you for your new life.

3. Claim a Sound Mind

To eliminate tormenting thoughts, claim the peace that is rightfully
yours. Jesus said:

Peace I leave with you, my peace I give unto you: not as the
world giveth give I unto you. Let not your heart be troubled,
neither let it be afraid (John 14:27).

Paul declared: *"And the peace of God, which passeth all understanding,*
shall keep your hearts and minds through Christ Jesus" (Phil. 4:7).

He also wrote under the inspiration of the Holy Spirit, *"Let this mind be in you, which was also in Christ Jesus"* (Phil. 2:5). The word *let* means "to permit" or "embrace" a mind, like that of Christ. Study the Gospels and you will see that Christ's mind was one set on destiny, purpose, and 100 percent victory. It was one of compassion and love.

4. *Take Wrong Thoughts Captive and Cast Them Down*

Bring *"...into captivity every thought to the obedience of Christ"* (2 Cor. 10:5). If thoughts were not enemies, then there would be no need to take them captive.

Think about how a soldier takes an enemy captive in the natural world. Apply these ideas spiritually as you take captive every thought.

Paul declared:

> *For though we walk in the flesh, we do not war after the flesh: (For the weapons of our warfare are not carnal, but mighty through God to the pulling down of strong holds;) Casting down imaginations, and every high thing that exalteth itself against the knowledge of God, and bringing into captivity every thought to the obedience of Christ* (2 Corinthians 10:3-5).

Cast down evil imaginations and bring every thought into captivity and obedience to the Lord. Consciously take control of your mind and refuse to dwell on the thoughts satan inserts. Note that *you* are told to cast down—it is not something God does for you.

5. *Think on the Good Things*

Ask God to change your thought patterns from negative to positive. Paul said:

> *Finally, brethren, whatsoever things are true, whatsoever things are honest, whatsoever things are just, whatsoever things are pure, whatsoever things are lovely, whatsoever things are of*

good report; if there be any virtue, and if there be any praise, think on these things (Philippians 4:8).

6. *Renew Your Mind*

Paul directed: *"And be renewed in the spirit of your mind"* (Eph. 4:23). He said to not be conformed to the world: *"...but be ye transformed by the renewing of your mind..."* (Rom. 12:2). You renew your mind by prayer and study and meditation in God's Word.

7. *Keep Your Mind Stayed on God*

Keep your mind centered on God instead of your problems and circumstances, and you will live your new life in perfect peace:

> *Thou wilt keep him in perfect peace, whose mind is stayed on Thee; because he trusteth in Thee* (Isaiah 26:3).

ARE YOU READY FOR A NEW BEGINNING?

Jesus spoke a new opinion over the adulterous woman's life. He is speaking a new opinion over your life right now. No matter what your circumstance, no matter how bad your past or present, you can have a new beginning.

Begin to agree with the new opinion God is speaking over your life. Don't speak words of defeat. Speak words of victory, declaring that you can do all things through Christ who strengthens you. (Read Philippians 4:13.)

Death and life are in the power of the tongue. Choose life, and begin to speak words that embrace your new life. (Read Proverbs 18:21.) James compares the tongue to the helm of a ship, a little thing yet it is the instrument that sets the course of a great vessel. (Read James 3:4.) Your words will establish the course of your destiny. Your own words will either catapult you into your new beginning or prevent you from entering into all God has for you.

Take time to act right now upon what you learned in this chapter. Bind the manifestation of satan's strategies in your mind:

- Discouragement

- Depression

- Wrong attitudes and emotions

- Rebellion

- Accusation and condemnation

- Fear

Take control of your mind by:

- Letting the Holy Spirit search your mind.

- Using your spiritual armor.

- Claiming a sound mind.

- Taking wrong thoughts captive and casting them down.

- Thinking about the good things.

CHAPTER 4

LIVING A CHANGED LIFE

Some people receive God's initial forgiveness at salvation, but then return to the old lifestyle. In Chapter 1, we learned that when Jesus granted new life to the woman caught in adultery He told her, "Go your way and sin no more." She was to live out her salvation through a changed life.

The Bible teaches that man is body, soul, and spirit. When you accept Christ as Savior, the change is a spiritual one. You experience a spiritual rebirth:

> *Jesus answered, Verily, verily, I say unto thee, Except a man be born of water and of the Spirit, he cannot enter into the kingdom of God. That which is born of the flesh is flesh; and that which is born of the Spirit is spirit. Marvel not that I said unto thee, Ye must be born again. The wind bloweth where it listeth, and thou hearest the sound thereof, but canst not tell whence it cometh, and whither it goeth: so is every one that is born of the Spirit* (John 3:5-8).

It is your spirit that is born again. You do not experience a physical change when you receive Christ. You don't become taller, shorter, heavier, or leaner. Your physical body does not change. Your spirit is born again by the Spirit of God.

After your new spiritual birth, your soul (which is your mind, will, and emotions) must be supernaturally changed as you live out this new life. For years your soul has ruled your spirit and your flesh. Whatever you desired, you did—whether it be drugs, alcohol, pornography, immorality, etc. You did not exercise control over emotions such as anger, unforgiveness, and bitterness. You went where you wanted to go and did what you wanted to do.

Repetition of sinful behavior leads to more of the same until certain actions are so entrenched in our lives that we cannot stop. We become enslaved to habitual sin and spiritual strongholds are erected.

This is what the apostle Paul struggled with after his conversion. He said:

> *For that which I do I allow not: for what I would, that do I not; but what I hate, that do I. If then I do that which I would not, I consent unto the law that it is good. Now then it is no more I that do it, but sin that dwelleth in me. For I know that in me (that is, in my flesh,) dwelleth no good thing: for to will is present with me; but how to perform that which is good I find not. For the good that I would I do not: but the evil which I would not, that I do. Now if I do that I would not, it is no more I that do it, but sin that dwelleth in me. I find then a law, that, when I would do good, evil is present with me (Romans 7:15-21).*

You cannot change your soulish nature on your own. Self-effort will not rid you of habitual sin. Paul found that out.

Addictions cannot be broken through self-effort. You must let God supernaturally change your soulish realm—your mind, will, and emotions. For years, your sinful soulish nature has controlled your body and your spirit. Now you must learn to let your redeemed spirit control your body and soul.

OPERATING IN THE FLESH

A prime example of a man who needed this supernatural change of his soulish nature is Jacob, whose story is recorded in the Book of Genesis. Most of Jacob's early life is a record of operating in the flesh, out of a soulish nature that needed supernatural change.

We are first introduced to Jacob at his birth in Genesis chapter 25. His mother, Rebekah, was carrying twins and felt the babies struggling within her. When she inquired of the Lord concerning this strange phenomena, He said:

> *...Two nations are in thy womb, and two manner of people shall be separated from thy bowels; and the one people shall be stronger than the other people; and the elder shall serve the younger. And when her days to be delivered were fulfilled, behold, there were twins in her womb. And the first came out red, all over like an hairy garment; and they called his name Esau. And after that came his brother out, and his hand took hold on Esau's heel; and his name was called Jacob: and Isaac was threescore years old when she bare them* (Genesis 25:23-26).

God declared that the descendants of these twins would become two nations, and from the start—even in the birthing process—these boys were struggling against one another in fierce competition.

Esau's descendants developed into the nation of Edom, while Jacob's descendants became the nation of Israel. The conflict between the brothers continued into adulthood and the nations that came from them were often at war with one another through the years (see Num. 20:14-21; 2 Sam. 8:13-14; 2 Kings 8:20-22).

Centuries later, the nation of Edom, which descended from Esau, was destroyed by decree of God (see Isaiah 34:5-6; 63:1; Obadiah 1-21; Malachi 1:3). Edom became a symbol of the godless people of the world who care little for spiritual things and are carnal, greedy, and treacherous.

These twin brothers were exact opposites. Esau loved the outdoors and was a cunning hunter. Jacob enjoyed remaining indoors. They even differed in appearance, with Esau being hairy and Jacob smooth-skinned. They grew up in a home divided by partiality, as Isaac favored Esau and Rebekah loved Jacob (see Gen. 25:27-28).

THE BIRTHRIGHT

The name *Jacob* means, "he that supplants or undermines." It certainly reflected his personality. His first notable act was stealing the birthright from his brother Esau.

Because he was the oldest son, Esau was entitled to receive the birthright—which, in ancient times, was an important and sacred thing. Through the birthright, the family name and titles were passed along to the eldest son. He would also receive a major portion of the inheritance.

The birthright represented more than just entitlement to the physical assets of a family. It was also a spiritual position and—in the case of Esau and Jacob—it meant that the one with the birthright would be the recipient of the covenant promise made to their grandfather, Abraham, and ultimately become an ancestor of the Messiah.

Esau was the firstborn and the birthright was legally his, but he failed to appreciate its value and sacredness. In a single moment of uncontrolled fleshly appetites, he lost it:

> *And Jacob sod pottage: and Esau came from the field, and he was faint: And Esau said to Jacob, Feed me, I pray thee, with that same red pottage; for I am faint: therefore was his name called Edom. And Jacob said, Sell me this day thy birthright. And Esau said, Behold, I am at the point to die: and what profit shall this birthright do to me? And Jacob said, Swear to me this day; and he sware unto him: and he sold his birthright unto Jacob. Then Jacob gave Esau bread and pottage of lentiles; and he did eat and drink, and rose up, and went his way: thus Esau despised his birthright* (Genesis 25:29-34).

For a mere pot of stew, Esau sold his birthright to Jacob, reflecting an attitude of disdain toward the things of God.

Some people wonder why God chose Jacob over Esau and declared before their birth that the elder would serve the younger. This incident answers that question. God had to choose between someone who thought so little of the birthright that he would sell it for a bowl of stew and a man who thought so much of it that he would manipulate in order to obtain it. In the New Testament, Esau is considered a profane person who foolishly squandered his life and God's blessings (see Heb. 12:16).

THE BLESSING

According to Jewish custom, as the oldest son Esau was also to receive the blessing from his father, Isaac. The paternal blessing was a prophetic promise of prosperity, power, and security that normally went to the oldest son. But before the birth of the twins, God had directed that the blessing should rest upon Jacob:

> *And not only this; but when Rebecca also had conceived by one, even by our father Isaac; (For the children being not yet born, neither having done any good or evil, that the purpose of God according to election might stand, not of works, but of him that calleth;) It was said unto her, The elder shall serve the younger* (Romans 9:10-12).

Although Isaac knew from the beginning that Jacob was to receive the blessing, he favored Esau and wanted to follow the customary tradition of giving it to him. One day, the aging Isaac directed Esau to go hunting and prepare him a meal of venison so that he could pass on the blessing before his death. (Read Genesis 27:1-4.)

Rebekah overheard this conversation and set in motion events that would enable Jacob to receive the blessing instead of Esau. She cooked some venison, helped Jacob disguise himself, and sent him in to Isaac:

> *And he* [Jacob] *came near, and kissed him: and he* [Isaac] *smelled the smell of his raiment, and blessed him, and said, See, the smell of my son is as the smell of a field which the Lord hath blessed: Therefore God give thee of the dew of heaven, and the fatness of the earth, and plenty of corn and*

wine: Let people serve thee, and nations bow down to thee: be Lord over thy brethren, and let thy mother's sons bow down to thee: cursed be every one that curseth thee, and blessed be he that blesseth thee (Genesis 27:27-29).

Shortly after Jacob departed, Esau came in with a savory dish of venison for his father:

And Isaac his father said unto him, Who art thou? And he said, I am thy son, thy firstborn Esau. And Isaac trembled very exceedingly, and said, Who? where is he that hath taken venison, and brought it me, and I have eaten of all before thou camest, and have blessed him? yea, and he shall be blessed. And when Esau heard the words of his father, he cried with a great and exceeding bitter cry, and said unto his father, Bless me, even me also, O my father. And he said, Thy brother came with subtlety, and hath taken away thy blessing (Genesis 27:32-35).

With these two events (the seizing of the birthright and the blessing), a pattern of habitual manipulative behavior was established in Jacob's life.

Shortly after these events, Esau determined he would kill Jacob. Rebekah overheard the plot and told Jacob to flee to his uncle Laban in Haran for a time. Rebekah would never see her favored son again. She would die before his return. (Read Genesis 27:41-46.)

BETHEL

On the way to Uncle Laban's, Jacob had what was the potential to be a life-changing experience:

And he lighted upon a certain place, and tarried there all night, because the sun was set; and he took of the stones of that place, and put them for his pillows, and lay down in that place to sleep. And he dreamed, and behold a ladder set up on the earth, and the top of it reached to heaven: and behold the angels of God ascending and descending on it. And, behold, the Lord stood above it, and said, I am the Lord God of Abraham thy father, and the God of Isaac: the land whereon thou liest, to thee will I give it, and to thy seed; And thy seed shall be as the dust of the earth, and thou shalt spread abroad to the west, and to the east, and to the north, and to the south: and in thee and in thy seed shall all the families of the earth be blessed. And, behold, I am with thee, and will keep thee in all places whither thou goest, and will bring thee again into this land; for I will not leave thee, until I have done that which I have spoken to thee of. And Jacob awaked out of his sleep, and he said, Surely the Lord is in this place; and I knew it not. And he was afraid, and said, How dreadful is this place! this is none other but the house of God, and this is the gate of heaven. And Jacob rose up early in the morning, and took the stone that he had put for his pillows, and set it up for a pillar, and poured oil upon the top of it. And he called the name of that place Bethel: but the name of that city was called Luz at the first. And Jacob vowed a vow, saying, If God will be with me, and will keep me in this way that I go, and will give me bread to eat, and raiment to put on, So that I come again to my father's house in peace; then shall the Lord be my God: And this stone, which I have set for a pillar, shall be God's house: and of all that Thou shalt give me I will surely give the tenth unto Thee (Genesis 28:11-22).

At Bethel, Jacob heard the voice of God and received tremendous promises from God, including:

- The promise of God's presence: *"...behold, I am with thee..."* (Gen. 28:15).

- The promise of protection: *"...and will keep thee in all places whither thou goest…"* (Gen. 28:15).

- The promise of direction: *"…and will bring thee again into this land…"* (Gen. 28:15).

- The pledge that God's purposes and promises would be fulfilled: *"…I will not leave thee, until I have done that which I have spoken to thee of"* (Gen. 28:15).

Jacob realized he was in the house of God, the very gate of Heaven. (Read Genesis 28:17-22.) He made vows and paid tithes. (Read Genesis 28:20-22.)

Jacob had a tremendous experience, but his life was not changed. He saw it as an opportunity to obtain his own selfish desires. He tried to bargain with God, asking Him to "bless me and my plans, give me my desires, give me peace, give me an inheritance." (Read Genesis 28:20-21.) He didn't get it yet: religion, rituals, and vows don't change you. Only God can change your fleshly nature.

God had already guaranteed the things Jacob was bargaining for, plus much more. He was groveling, begging, and manipulating to obtain what God had already promised. Jacob was still bound by the stronghold of his flesh, his habitual manipulation. The potential for a breakthrough was there, but Jacob did not avail himself of it.

Through the pages of this book, God is bringing you to your own Bethel and giving you an opportunity for a new beginning. He has provided all the resources of Heaven to give you victory over your habitual sins, your addictions, and the spiritual strongholds of the enemy. Will you continue to struggle in your own flesh, as did Jacob, or will you be changed by yielding to God?

THE PATTERN CONTINUES

At Bethel, Jacob had the opportunity for a spiritual breakthrough, but he did not avail himself of it. He had a religious experience, but a religious experience will not change your life. You must have supernatural change through the power of Almighty God.

Over the next few years, Jacob continued his manipulative, sinful behavior as he constantly bargained with and tried to outwit his Uncle Laban. Jacob set his eyes on beautiful Rachel, whose family heritage was one of deceit and idolatry. Deceived by Uncle Laban, Jacob ended up with two wives—Leah and Rachel—and constant conflict in his home. Eventually, after overhearing Laban's disgruntled sons plotting against him, Jacob took his family and fled Haran.

Jacob's problem was that he wanted to control his own life, and he continually manipulated people and circumstances to do it. Habitual manipulation became a way of life for him, and it resulted in a spiritual stronghold that caused continual problems.

If you are to receive the new beginning God has for you, your fleshly nature must be changed. The chains of your habitual sins and addictions must be conquered. Like Jacob, you must experience a breakthrough.

JACOB'S BREAKTHROUGH AT JABBOK

Fleeing from Haran, Jacob decided to return home to Canaan. On the way, he and his family camped at a place called *Jabbok*, which means, "a place of passing over," "change," "breakthrough," and "a sudden advancement." Here, for the first time on record, Jacob admitted that he needed God's help. He declared:

> *...O God of my father Abraham, and God of my father Isaac, the Lord which saidst unto me, Return unto thy country, and to thy kindred, and I will deal well with thee: I am not worthy of the least of all the mercies, and of all the truth, which thou hast shewed unto thy servant; for with my staff I passed over this Jordan; and now I am become two bands. Deliver me, I pray thee, from the hand of my brother, from the hand of Esau: for I fear him, lest he will come and smite me, and the mother with the children* (Genesis 32:9-11).

Then Jacob came alone to Jabbok—the place of breakthrough, where everything changed:

And he rose up that night, and took his two wives, and his two womenservants, and his eleven sons, and passed over the ford Jabbok. And he took them, and sent them over the brook, and sent over that he had. And Jacob was left alone; and there wrestled a man with him until the breaking of the day. And when he saw that he prevailed not against him, he touched the hollow of his thigh; and the hollow of Jacob's thigh was out of joint, as he wrestled with him. And he said, Let me go, for the day breaketh. And he said, I will not let thee go, except thou bless me. And he said unto him, What is thy name? And he said, Jacob. And he said, Thy name shall be called no more Jacob, but Israel: for as a prince hast thou power with God and with men, and hast prevailed. And Jacob asked him, and said, Tell me, I pray thee, thy name. And he said, Wherefore is it that thou dost ask after my name? And he blessed him there. And Jacob called the name of the place Peniel: for I have seen God face to face, and my life is preserved. And as he passed over Penuel the sun rose upon him, and he halted upon his thigh. Therefore the children of Israel eat not of the sinew which shrank, which is upon the hollow of the thigh, unto this day: because he touched the hollow of Jacob's thigh in the sinew that shrank (Genesis 32:22-32).

Jacob was left alone. Have you ever felt that way? When you are left alone, it is usually for a purpose. God is getting ready to do something in your life. Quit trying to fit in with the crowd. God puts you in isolation to birth divine revelation. John on Patmos Island is a case in point. It was there, in isolation, where John received one of the greatest prophetic revelations regarding the end times recorded in the Bible.

Here at Jabbok, Jacob was at the end of his natural resources. Behind him was an angry Laban and ahead of him was a vengeful Esau. When you are "between a rock and hard place," and it seems you have no options in the natural world, that is when God can finally get your attention.

The Bible records that a man appeared and wrestled with Jacob throughout the night. We learn later that this was a spiritual being, presumed to be the incarnate Christ. As dawn approached, He touched Jacob's thigh and the sinew shrank, leaving him with a permanent limp. All his life, Jacob had run. He had run from Esau, from Laban, from Canaan, and from Haran, so God crippled his greatest natural strength so that he would rely upon God instead of on his flesh.

This is an example of how your life must change. You must quit struggling in the natural, and let God supernaturally affect change in your life. God will wrestle with you until He accomplishes His purposes in you. He will wrestle with your wrong attitudes, habits, and addictions. He will be there through the darkness of the night until dawn breaks and you receive your deliverance.

Jacob discovered that you don't enter into the blessing of new life by wrestling for it, but by clinging to God and allowing the new life to be lived out through His power. God knows how to touch you so you will stop running and start clinging.

God also gave Jacob a new name. As mentioned previously, Jacob's name meant "he that supplants or undermines." Every time someone called his name, it reflected his old nature, and the spiritual strongholds of his fleshly life. So God gave him a new name—*Israel*—which means "a prince who has power with God and man." From that point on, Jacob's life was different. He wasn't perfect, but his basic, fleshly nature changed.

YOUR IDENTITY MUST CHANGE

God asked Jacob his name. It was not because He didn't already know it but to force Jacob to admit his spiritual condition. He was a manipulator, one who undermined and supplanted others.

Like Jacob, your identity must change. Your deliverance comes by honestly facing your anger, addiction, bitterness, unforgiveness, or habitual sin. After receiving Jesus Christ, your lifestyle must change. You cannot return to the old life. You cannot remain bound in sins, addictions, and habits, but neither can you change yourself. Your soulish nature cannot change through rehabilitation or self-effort. You cannot manipulate yourself into this new life. It will only come as God supernaturally changes your identity.

God has given you power over all the power of the enemy. (Read Luke 10:19.) He has given you the power to live a changed life:

> But as many as received Him, to them gave He power to become the sons of God, even to them that believe on His name: Which were born, not of blood, nor of the will of the flesh, nor of the will of man, but of God (John 1:12-13).

God wants to give you a supernatural revelation of the tremendous spiritual resources available to enable you to live a victorious life:

> That the God of our Lord Jesus Christ, the Father of glory, may give unto you the spirit of wisdom and revelation in the knowledge of him: The eyes of your understanding being enlightened; that ye may know what is the hope of His calling, and what the riches of the glory of His inheritance in the saints, And what is the exceeding greatness of His power to us-ward who believe, according to the working of His mighty power (Ephesians 1:17-19).

YOUR NEW LIFE AWAITS

God was continually at work in Jacob's life, despite his many failures. God is at work in your life also, despite your failures. You can be *"...confident of this very thing, that He which hath begun a good work in you will perform it until the day of Jesus Christ"* (Phil. 1:6).

Jacob wasted years before claiming the spiritual inheritance God had already provided for him back at Bethel. Near the end of his life, Jacob's sad commentary was:

> The days of the years of my pilgrimage are an hundred and thirty years: few and evil have the days of the years of my

life been, and have not attained unto the days of the years of the life of my fathers in the days of their pilgrimage (Genesis 47:9).

Don't waste years, like Jacob did, going your own way, struggling in the flesh, bound by spiritual strongholds of sin, addiction, and negative emotions. Your new life awaits you right now! Stop wrestling and start clinging. Accept your new identity from God, turn your back on the past, and begin to experience a changed life.

God also wants to give you a new vision that will provide focus for your new life. More about that in the next chapter.

CHAPTER 5

RECEIVING A NEW VISION

The Bible states in Proverbs 29:18: *"Where there is no vision, the people perish...."*

All over the world there are born-again believers who are perishing. They are not perishing in sin. They have accepted salvation through Jesus Christ, they attend church services, read the Bible, and may even be leaders in the Church. But they are dying spiritually. Their lives as believers are routine. They have lost sight of their divine destiny. They have no vision and they need a new beginning.

This book describes specific areas in which God wants to give you a new beginning, but to receive this revelation you must first have spiritual vision. You must be given the ability to see into the spirit world and know that things can change. You must grasp your divine purpose and destiny.

WHY SPIRITUAL VISION?

What is spiritual vision? Why is it important?

Perhaps the best example is found in the story of the prophet Elisha and his servant Gehazi recorded in Second Kings 6:15-17. God's people, Israel, were surrounded by the enemy nation of Syria. There were many soldiers, horses, and chariots of war.

When Elisha's servant, Gehazi, saw the great force of the enemy he was afraid. He cried out to Elisha, What shall we do? Elisha told him: *"Fear not, for they that be with us are more than they that be with them"* (2 Kings 6:16). Then Elisha prayed that God would open Gehazi's eyes and allow him to see in the spirit world.

The request was granted, and Gehazi saw the spiritual forces of God surrounding Israel, which were greater than those of the enemy.

Without spiritual vision, you cannot see beyond the natural circumstances of life. You cannot see your finances improving, your relationships mended, or your body healed. Without supernatural understanding, you will not be able to grasp the truths revealed in this book—that God really can give you a new beginning in every area of your life.

Without spiritual vision, you will be defeated by the powers of the enemy that you see at work in the natural world around you. Your vision will remain focused on your problems and your life will become a cycle of crying out, "What shall I do?"

You won't get to where you are going by accident. Your new beginning just won't happen. You must purpose in your heart and grasp the vision of your new beginning.

WHAT IS SPIRITUAL VISION?

Spiritual vision involves seeing beyond the natural world into the spiritual world. It is understanding the divine purpose of God and recognizing your part in His plan. Spiritual vision provides a clear image of the life God intends for you and then directs every step of your Christian life toward achieving it.

A good example is the apostle Paul, who declared: *"...I was not disobedient unto the heavenly vision"* (Acts 26:19). The heavenly (spiritual) vision God gave Paul became the compelling force in his life. God told him:

> *But rise, and stand upon thy feet: for I have appeared unto thee for this purpose, to make thee a minister and a witness both of these things which thou hast seen, and of those things in the which I will appear unto thee; Delivering thee from the people, and from the Gentiles, unto whom now I send thee, To*

open their eyes, and to turn them from darkness to light, and from the power of Satan unto God, that they may receive forgiveness of sins, and inheritance among them which are sanctified by faith that is in me (Acts 26:16-18).

God gave Paul spiritual vision for the purpose of making him a minister and witness to the Gentiles. God gave Paul a plan to achieve the vision. Paul was to open their spiritual eyes from darkness to light, turn them from the power of satan to God, lead them to forgiveness of sins, and reveal their spiritual inheritance made possible by faith.

God wants to give you a spiritual vision just as He did Paul. He also wants to reveal the plan that will enable you to fulfill your destiny. As you experience new vision, you will become a participator instead of a mere spectator in God's divine plan.

The natural birth process that brings a human baby into the world is similar to the process of the birth of a vision in the spirit world. When God conceives a new vision in your spirit, there will be a time of development. The vision must become a vital, living part of you. It must draw from your own life source as well as from the divine source that conceived it.

As in the delivery of a child, spiritual vision will be birthed by intense mental, physical, and spiritual concentration. In the natural world, labor (travail) is an intense time. During labor, there comes a time of transition. It is the most difficult time, right before the child is born.

It is at this point in the spiritual world that many have lost their vision. The difficulties caused them to abandon their dream, to back off from their divine destiny. They lose hope that things can change, that their relationships can be healed, that their finances improve, or that their ministry advances.

Transition means "change." As God gives you the spiritual vision for your new beginning, it will require change in your life. It will call for new commitment and dedication. You may experience pressure in every area of your life. Everything within you may cry out for relief from the spiritual birth pangs of what God is bringing forth.

This is the point where many fail. Repeatedly, God has brought His people to the time of transition in order to birth new things, but because the transition was too difficult many have turned back. They could not take the pressure of this most difficult time. It required changes in their thought patterns and lifestyle that they were not willing to make. They could not abandon self-effort and tradition. They could not set aside their own ambitions and desires to embrace the plan of God.

Travail is a painful experience, but it is only through travail that the vision can be birthed:

> *Who hath heard such a thing? who hath seen such things? Shall the earth be made to bring forth in one day? or shall a nation be born at once? for as soon as Zion travailed, she brought forth her children. Shall I bring to the birth, and not cause to bring forth? saith the Lord: shall I cause to bring forth, and shut the womb? saith thy God* (Isaiah 66:8-9).

God wants you to receive the vision of the new beginning He has for you in every area of your life. He wants to bring forth divine purpose and birth something great through you. He wants to give you a new life!

Birth requires change. In the natural world, the child must leave the security of the womb. When you were born again you had to leave the old life of sin. You had to let Jesus change your thought and action patterns.

To give birth to new life spiritually also requires change. It requires courage to step from the known into the unknown. Are you ready to receive new spiritual vision? Are you willing to experience spiritual travail in order to birth something new and vital in your Christian life?

THE VISION OF ABRAHAM

God gave Abraham an amazing vision, one that required a tremendous act of faith. He asked him to step out into an unknown future with nothing more than a promise from God:

> *Now the Lord had said unto Abram, Get thee out of thy country, and from thy kindred, and from thy father's house,*

unto a land that I will shew thee: And I will make of thee a great nation, and I will bless thee, and make thy name great; and thou shalt be a blessing (Genesis 12:1-2).

The vision that God gave to Abraham would result in him being blessed and being a blessing. The new things God wants to bring forth in your life are not only to bless you, but to make you a blessing to others.

The writer of Hebrews declares: *"By faith Abraham, when he was called to go out into a place which he should after receive for an inheritance, obeyed; and he went out, not knowing whither he went"* (Heb. 11:8).

The Lord didn't lay out a detailed travel plan for Abraham. God didn't provide an explanation of the dangers that might be involved, the changes required, or a detailed description of the Promised Land. Abraham went out at God's promises to show him and bless him. He told Abraham that he would be a blessing.

If you are to embrace a new beginning in your life, then you must do likewise. You must receive the vision that God has a new beginning for you, and you must rise up to embrace it.

You may not understand how God will heal your relationships. You may not know how your finances will ever change. You cannot see how your ministry will be restored. But at God's Word, you must believe and begin to act upon His Word in faith.

God gave Abraham another tremendous promise, that he would be the father of many nations. But there was one major problem: his wife was barren. So Abraham tried to bring forth his God-given vision through self-effort by the birth of Ishmael. He knew God wanted to make him a great nation and he thought an heir could not come through his wife, Sarah.

So he did something about it. He had relations with Sarah's servant girl Hagar, and Ishmael was born. Whose power was behind Ishmael, that of Abraham or that of God? Was the fulfillment of the vision through Ishmael man-made or God-made?

You can bring an Ishmael on the scene through your own efforts. *Ishmael* represents your plans, methods, and natural abilities. The heavenly vision was represented by Isaac. It must be birthed by God. Your new beginning will not be birthed by human effort. It will be birthed by God Himself.

Scripture has no record of God speaking again to Abraham for 13 years after the birth of Ishmael. Not until it was humanly impossible for Abraham to have a child did God again stir the vision within him. By then, self-effort had died.

Then came the birth of a vision, for in the perfect timing of God, Isaac was miraculously born. But with the birth of God's plan (Isaac), Ishmael (self-effort) must be cast out. It is time for your Isaac (God's plan) to be birthed in your spirit. In order for this to happen, Ishmael must be cast out. You may have tried in the past and failed. Now it is time to cast out your self-effort and embrace God's plan.

It is a painful experience to cast out self-effort, your plans, ambitions, traditions, and programs. God is saying to you, as He did to Abraham, "Grieve not for Ishmael (self-effort), for in Isaac shall your seed be called." In Isaac, the source of the vision was God.

This book is not a self-help or a how-to book. It is a revelation that God wants to give you a new start in every area of your life. This new beginning will not come through self-effort, but through divine birth.

THE VISION OF JOSEPH

You will experience many challenges as you rise up to embrace your new beginning. Satan wants to abort your future. He wants to keep you in the pit of negative circumstances where you are at present.

In the Book of Genesis, the Bible tells the story of a young man who had a difficult journey to the fulfillment of his vision. You can read the story of Joseph in Genesis chapters 30-50.

Joseph's home environment was anything but pleasant. His father, Jacob, had a history of deception. His mother, Rachel, was continually in conflict with Jacob's other wife, Leah. Rachel was always trying to manipulate Jacob and gain his exclusive affection.

There was partiality in the home, which created rivalry and jealousy. Jacob preferred Rachel to Leah and Joseph to the rest of his sons. The special coat given to Joseph by his father was more than just a beautiful garment. It was not a work garment like shepherds wore so it set Joseph apart as the favored child, one who would not work as his brothers did.

God gave Joseph a vision of the future, and his brothers hated him for it. (Read Genesis 37:8.) They could not even speak peaceably to him. (Read Genesis chapter 37.) Joseph's brothers were also involved in a terrible sin of immorality at Shechem. (Read Genesis chapter 37.)

Joseph lived in a family that was dominated by deceit, immorality, manipulation, envy, and hatred. For 17 years he was raised in this dysfunctional family. He could have blamed this environment for ruining his life and, in so doing, thrown away his future.

You may be able to identify with Joseph if you came from a home where you suffered abuse or abandonment. The question is, will you let the pain of your past abort the future God has planned for you?

Joseph's early environment was not the only difficulty he encountered on the way to his destiny. In Genesis chapter 37, we learn how Joseph's brothers stripped him of his coat of many colors and threw him in a pit. Then they sat down, cold and uncaring, their ears deaf to his cries.

Can you identify with this? Have you been crying for help, with no answer from those around you? Little did Joseph think that he would someday look back on this great tragedy as the most significant event in God's plan for his life. The same may be true for you. The tragic situation you have experienced can be the door to your destiny. In Joseph's life, this pit led to the palace!

When an Egyptian caravan passed by, Joseph's brothers sold him into slavery. In Genesis chapter 39, you can read how Joseph suffered another ordeal when he was falsely accused of immorality and thrown into prison. But in every setback, the Lord was with Joseph. (Read Genesis 39:3.)

God has been with you also, in that dysfunctional family and in the tragic experiences of your past. He has not abandoned you. He has a future for you, a destiny and a hope.

Confinement is hard at any age, but Joseph was young and used to roaming the hillsides of Judea. Yet he refused to give in to despair. In Genesis chapters 39-40, we learn that he was placed in a position of responsibility in the prison and ministered to a butler and baker who were confined with him, both of whom promptly forgot him when they were released.

Humanly speaking, Joseph had every right to develop a negative attitude. Family and friends failed him, he was falsely accused and forgotten. But little did he know that every circumstance was bringing him nearer to his God-given destiny. This is what God is doing in your life also. Every event in your painful past can be used by God to help you achieve your destiny.

Eventually, the butler remembered Joseph and, along with Pharaoh, was used by God to elevate him to his destiny. God will send "butlers" and "Pharaohs" into your life also. These are men and women who will assist you on your way to a new beginning. Watch for them along your path.

Joseph was released from prison, became ruler of Egypt, and saved the then-known world from death through famine. Negative experiences of your past cannot abort God's purpose for your life unless you allow it by holding on to bitterness and unforgiveness.

When Joseph married, the names he gave his two children were symbolic of the experiences he had passed through. (Read Genesis 41:51-52.) The first child was named *Manasseh*, meaning, "God hath made me forget all my toil and all my father's house." Joseph didn't forget his father's house, but he forgot the pain associated with the events. You may never forget the difficulties of the past, but God wants to heal you of the pain of these experiences.

Joseph's second son was named *Ephraim*, meaning, "God hath caused me to be fruitful in the land of my affliction." Joseph was fruitful in affliction because he let God heal him of the pain of his past.

The only way you can receive a new beginning is to let go of the past, release unforgiveness and bitterness, and allow God to heal your pain. You must deal with the past before you can experience a fruitful future and embrace your new beginning.

Joseph went through many difficulties, but God used them all. Joseph was being prepared to save a nation. What great thing does God have planned for you? How will He use the experiences of your past as you submit them to Him?

When Joseph's brothers stood before him in Egypt, they didn't even recognize him. Joseph declared:

And Joseph said unto his brethren, Come near to me, I pray you. And they came near. And he said, I am Joseph your brother, whom ye sold into Egypt. Now therefore be not grieved, nor angry with yourselves, that ye sold me hither: for God did send me before you to preserve life. For these two years hath the famine been in the land: and yet there are five years, in the which there shall neither be earing nor harvest. And God sent me before you to preserve you a posterity in the earth, and to save your lives by a great deliverance. So now it was not you that sent me hither, but God: and he hath made me a father to Pharaoh, and lord of all his house, and a ruler throughout all the land of Egypt (Genesis 45:4-8).

Joseph realized that the painful events of his past were not just tough luck or unfortunate circumstances. He declared: *"But as for you, ye thought evil against me; but God meant it unto good, to bring to pass, as it is this day, to save much people alive"* (Gen. 50:20).

As a child, Joseph had dreams and visions of being in a place of responsibility and authority. All through the long, difficult years, Joseph never lost that dream. When at last he stood in the place of his God-appointed destiny, he remembered the dream: *"And Joseph remembered the dreams which he dreamed"* (Gen. 42:9).

God has a plan for your life and a destiny for your future. Don't let the pain of your past abort your future. Don't let it hinder your new beginning. Don't be afraid to step out by faith and embrace the revelation that things can change. God is restoring your vision for a new future and a fresh beginning. He also wants to rekindle your lost dreams. The next chapter will explain exactly how He will do it.

CHAPTER 6

REKINDLING LOST DREAMS

His name was John. He loved God. He had a dream. In fact, it was more than a dream. He knew that it was a sacred calling. John wanted to serve on the mission field to share the Gospel of the Lord Jesus Christ. He studied and prepared diligently, and then one day, his big break came. He was asked to accompany a mission team to the field. His dream had come true! He was to serve God as a missionary.

Once he got to the mission field, things got tough. Hours were long. Accommodations were primitive. The receptivity of the people in some cities was nil. In some places, the ministry team was actually run out of town! Often, they were in peril and hunger.

Somewhere along the way, John got discouraged and returned home. His dream of ministry was abandoned.

HIS STORY IS NOT UNIQUE

We are talking about John Mark, whose story is recorded in the Book of Acts. His experience is not unique. There are many believers who once had a dream, a calling, a vision, and a divine purpose, yet somewhere along the way, they abandoned it.

God wants to restore your lost dream. He wants to give you new purpose and direction. He wants to pick up the shattered pieces of your ministry and launch you out into the harvest field once again. No matter how you may have failed, He will give you another chance.

In Acts 12:25, we read where the ministry team of Saul and Barnabas... returned from Jerusalem, when they had fulfilled their ministry, and took with them John, whose surname was *Mark*.

We are not told the details of John Mark's problems, but in Pamphylia this young man abandoned the ministry team and returned home.

In Acts chapter 15 when Paul and Barnabas were planning another journey, they were at odds over the young man:

> *And Barnabas determined to take with them John, whose surname was Mark. But Paul thought not good to take him with them, who departed from them from Pamphylia, and went not with them to the work. And the contention was so sharp between them, that they departed asunder one from the other: and so Barnabas took Mark, and sailed unto Cyprus; And Paul chose Silas, and departed, being recommended by the brethren unto the grace of God. And he went through Syria and Cilicia, confirming the churches* (Acts 15:37-41).

For some reason, John Mark left the ministry team in Pamphylia. When Paul and Barnabas were planning their next trip, Barnabas wanted to give John Mark another chance, but Paul refused. The contention became so great that the men decided to go separate directions. Paul teamed up with Silas, and Barnabas took John Mark with him.

NOW PROFITABLE

Thank the Lord for men and women like Barnabas, who grasp the true meaning of reconciliation and reflect God's nature by giving defeated believers another chance!

We are not told the details of how Barnabas discipled John Mark, but we know that this young man (at one time deemed a deserter and a failure) became a valued minister of God. When Paul was facing his final days, he wrote to Timothy asking for John Mark. Paul said:

> *For I am now ready to be offered, and the time of my departure is at hand. I have fought a good fight, I have finished my course, I have kept the faith: Henceforth there is laid up for me a crown of righteousness, which the Lord, the righteous judge, shall give me at that day: and not to me only, but unto all them also that love His appearing. Do thy diligence to come shortly unto me: For Demas hath forsaken me, having loved this present world, and is departed unto Thessalonica; Crescens to Galatia, Titus unto Dalmatia. Only Luke is with me. Take Mark, and bring him with thee: for he is profitable to me for the ministry* (2 Timothy 4:6-11).

One simple sentence in this passage confirms John Mark's new beginning: *"Take Mark, bring him with you, for he is profitable for the ministry"* (2 Tim. 4:11).

How that phrase must have echoed in John Mark's heart: He is profitable. He is profitable. He is profitable.

Perhaps you can see yourself in John Mark in that God gave you a dream—vision, ministry, calling—that you have abandoned. Perhaps difficult circumstances caused you to turn your back and walk away. Maybe it was disillusionment with people. Perhaps you were deeply hurt by someone.

Whatever your reason, whatever your past failure, God wants to rekindle your shattered dreams and set you back on the road to your divine destiny. He is speaking the same words over your life that Paul spoke over John Mark: You are profitable! You have a place in God's Kingdom! You have a work to do! Your dream can be restored!

REKINDLED DREAMS

John Mark is a tremendous example of how God wants to take shattered dreams, visions, and ministries and restore them. There is another great example in the Bible, and that is Moses, whose story provides spiritual principles that will help rekindle our own dreams.

The story of Moses' early life and calling is recorded in the first chapters of the Book of Exodus. Moses was born at a time of great peril when the ruling Pharaoh was having Israeli male babies killed in an attempt to thwart population growth and a potential rebellion in the Israelite community. Moses' mother attempted to hide him, but he was found by Pharaoh's daughter who raised him as her own son.

In an act of divine providence, Moses' own mother became his nursemaid. As he grew, she undoubtedly taught him of his Israeli heritage and about the things of God. This is evident in his response as a young adult when he witnessed an Egyptian beating an Israelite. Moses knew slavery was wrong. He most likely already had the dream and divine call of delivering his people when he witnessed this violent scene.

Moses responded in anger and killed the Egyptian taskmaster. Then, knowing his life was in danger for this act, Moses fled to the backside of the desert. For 40 long years, Moses lived with the memory of an aborted dream. He had tried and failed. Would God ever use him again?

Have you been there? Are you there right now? You stepped out to do what God called you to do, only to fail. Have you, like Moses, retreated to the desert to nurse your broken heart and your shattered dream?

One day, while watching a flock of sheep in the desert, Moses saw a burning bush that, miraculously, was not consumed. He drew near, and God spoke to him.

> *Now Moses kept the flock of Jethro his father in law, the priest of Midian: and he led the flock to the backside of the desert, and came to the mountain of God, even to Horeb. And the angel of the Lord appeared unto him in a flame of fire out of the midst of a bush: and he looked, and, behold, the bush burned with fire, and the bush was not consumed. And Moses said, I will now turn aside, and see this great sight, why the bush is not burnt. And when the Lord saw that he turned aside to see, God called unto him out of the midst of the bush,*

and said, Moses, Moses. And he said, Here am I. And he said, Draw not nigh hither: put off thy shoes from off thy feet, for the place whereon thou standest is holy ground. Moreover he said, I am the God of thy father, the God of Abraham, the God of Isaac, and the God of Jacob. And Moses hid his face; for he was afraid to look upon God. And the Lord said, I have surely seen the affliction of My people which are in Egypt, and have heard their cry by reason of their taskmasters; for I know their sorrows; And I am come down to deliver them out of the hand of the Egyptians, and to bring them up out of that land unto a good land and a large, unto a land flowing with milk and honey; unto the place of the Canaanites, and the Hittites, and the Amorites, and the Perizzites, and the Hivites, and the Jebusites. Now therefore, behold, the cry of the children of Israel is come unto Me: and I have also seen the oppression wherewith the Egyptians oppress them. Come now therefore, and I will send thee unto Pharaoh, that thou mayest bring forth My people the children of Israel out of Egypt (Exodus 3:1-10).

God knew exactly where Moses was, there in the backside of the desert. He had not forgotten him. God used the burning bush to rekindle his dreams. Neither has God abandoned you in the desert of your failure. He has not left you to die unfulfilled.

God knows right where you are, just as He did Moses. The words you are reading right now can become your "burning bush" if you will receive them. You can rise up again, empowered by God, and fulfill your dream, your ministry, your divine calling.

THREE STEPS TO REKINDLING YOUR DREAM

There are three major principles revealed in this story of Moses that, when applied in your own life, will rekindle your dream:

1. Reject Reasons for Remaining Where You Are

Moses had a multitude of reasons why he couldn't embrace his abandoned dream. First, he argued, "Who am I?"

> *And Moses said unto God, Who am I, that I should go unto Pharaoh, and that I should bring forth the children of Israel out of Egypt?* (Exodus 3:11)

Like Moses, many of us struggle with past failures and a lack of skills and abilities. God's answer to Moses was, "It is not who *you* are, but who *I am!*" It is not who you are that will bring forth your ministry, but who He is! You must act on the basis of who He is, not who you are.

Then Moses said, "I don't have the authority. Who will I say sent me?"

> *And Moses said unto God, Behold, when I come unto the children of Israel, and shall say unto them, The God of your fathers hath sent me unto you; and they shall say to me, What is His name? what shall I say unto them?* (Exodus 3:13)

God's answer to Moses was: *"Thus shalt thou say unto the children of Israel, I AM hath sent me unto you"* (Exod. 3:14).

God has already given you authority and power over the enemy:

> *Behold, I give unto you power to tread on serpents and scorpions, and over all the power of the enemy: and nothing shall by any means hurt you.* (Luke 10:19)

You have the power and authority of God to walk into your destiny and fulfill it.

Next, Moses objected. What if they don't believe me?

> *And Moses answered and said, But, behold, they will not believe me, nor hearken unto my voice: for they will say, The Lord hath not appeared unto thee* (Exodus 4:1).

God's answer to this objection was: *"…What is that in thine hand?…"* (Exod. 4:2). In Moses' hand was a rod, which represented God's power. Later on, this same rod was thrown down before Pharaoh and miracles happened, it was stretched over the Red Sea and the waters parted, and it brought forth water from a rock.

God is asking you the same question today: What is in your hand? You have talents, abilities, gifts, and skills that God can use if you will simply pick them up and begin to use them once again: *"For the gifts and calling of God are without repentance"* (Rom. 11:29).

Then Moses questioned, "What shall I say?" God responded, *"I will be with your mouth and teach you what you shall say"* (Exod. 4:12 NKJV). God's Word to you today is, *"The word is nigh thee, even in thy mouth, and in thy heart: that is, the word of faith, which we preach"* (Rom. 10:8).

In order to rekindle his aborted ministry, Moses had to eliminate all excuses. If you are to fulfill your destiny, you must do the same. Every reason you have that says why you can't, must go. You must eliminate them, one by one, in the name of Jesus!

You may have committed adultery. It is not the unpardonable sin. You can be forgiven and restored, as was King David.

You may be serving a life sentence in prison and wonder how you can have a new beginning. Your circumstance of incarceration may not change, but you can change. You can find a new destiny, a new purpose for living. Participate in the prison ministry. Reach out to young offenders serving short sentences. Mentor them so they will not return back to prison. Write, sing, teach, counsel, mentor someone.

No matter where you are or what your circumstances, begin right now to speak the Word of God over your lost vision, your shattered dream. Declare this truth: *"I can do all things through Christ which strengtheneth me"* (Phil. 4:13).

2. Rise up and Take Action

You must act on the Word of God or otherwise you will remain right where you are—in seclusion in your spiritual desert. Moses rose up and returned to Egypt to fulfill his dream.

After Saul's death, God told Samuel to stop grieving, get up, and go anoint a new king. God told Noah to rise up and build an ark. He told Nehemiah, arise and build! He said arise to a lame man by the side of the road. After Moses died, God told Joshua to rise up and take his position as leader of Israel.

If you are still sorrowing over your lost ministry and your shattered dream, then it is time to stop. Get up and begin to act in faith. You must make a change, or a year from now you will be right where you are today. God's Word to you is:

> ARISE [from the depression and prostration in which circum-
> stances have kept you—rise to a new life]! Shine (be radiant
> with the glory of the Lord), for your light is come, and the glory
> of the Lord is risen upon you! (Isaiah 60:1 AMP)

3. Rely on God's Power to Rekindle Your Dream

God told Moses, *"So I will stretch out My hand and strike Egypt with all My wonders which I will do in its midst; and after that he will let you go"* (Exod. 3:20 NKJV).

Moses' first attempt to deliver Israel was through human effort when in anger he killed the Egyptian. His efforts failed, and he fled to the dessert.

You tried in your flesh and failed. That is why your dream was shattered and your ministry abandoned. Now it is time to step forth in faith and let God birth through you new dreams, new visions, and new ministries.

From the sacred ground of the burning bush, Moses returned to Egypt and fulfilled his calling. His shattered dream became a reality as Israel was delivered from their cruel taskmasters and he led them to freedom.

THE BUSH STILL BURNS

A spiritual bush is burning for you right now. Its message is the same: God isn't through with you, despite your past failures. Your destiny is not the wilderness where you are right now. Your destiny is the dream God has placed within you, the calling that refuses to die, no matter how you try to forget it.

Take off your shoes right now as an act of submission and begin to praise God. Let those tears of repentance and submission flow. You are standing on holy ground. Your dream is being rekindled.

Like John Mark and Moses, God is giving you a new beginning in ministry, and this time you will not fail! Not only can you experience this new start in your ministry, but you can claim a new beginning for your entire family. Keep reading.

CHAPTER 7

CLAIMING A NEW FUTURE FOR YOUR FAMILY

We are living in an era of fractured families. There are absentee dads and moms, single parents, children killing children, rebellion, abuse, youths involved in gangs, addictions to drugs and alcohol. It gives new meaning to the term *dysfunctional family.*

Before you start this chapter, settle this in your heart: No matter what the situation in your family, you can have a new beginning. You can claim a new future for the dysfunctional family in which you now live. You can claim that mate for Jesus and salvation for your children and grandchildren. No matter what the past has been in your family and despite the present, the future can be different. You can claim a new future for your family.

One of the greatest stories illustrating a new beginning for a family is found in Joshua chapters 2-6. Take time to read this account before you continue with this chapter. From these passages we learn that the Israelites' journey from Egypt to Canaan, detailed in the Books of Exodus through Deuteronomy, concluded as the people reached their destination. They were camping on the eastern side of the Jordan River, on the plains of Moab, just north of the Dead Sea. They were poised and ready to enter their Promised Land.

Upon the death of Moses, Joshua had assumed leadership of God's people to direct the occupation of their Promised Land of Canaan. As a first step,

Joshua dispatched two spies to survey the fortified city of Jericho, the first target of their invasion. Unlike the venture of the 12 spies recorded in Numbers chapter 13, the objective of this mission was not to determine whether they should enter Canaan, but when and how it should be done.

Jericho, the ancient city of palms to which the spies were sent, was a prosperous and populous city surrounded by two great walls. According to archaeological findings, there was a space of 12 to 15 feet between these walls. Timbers were laid from one wall to the other and houses of sun-dried bricks were constructed to bridge the space between them.

Built over this gap between the two walls of Jericho was the house of a woman named Rahab who was a harlot. There was a constant stream of visitors in and out of her house and this probably influenced the spies to seek refuge there. They presumed that two strangers would not be noticed, but their presence did not go undetected:

> *And it was told the king of Jericho, saying, Behold, men have come here tonight from the children of Israel to search out the country. So the king of Jericho sent to Rahab, saying, Bring out the men who have come to you, who have entered your house, for they have come to search out all the country* (Joshua 2:2-3 NKJV).

Rahab took the men to the roof of her house and hid them with stalks of flax that were laid out for drying and processing. When the king's messengers arrived she told them:

> *Yes, the men came to me, but I did not know where they were from. And it happened as the gate was being shut, when it was dark, that the men went out. Where the men went I do not know; pursue them quickly, for you may overtake them* (Joshua 2:4-5 NKJV).

After the departure of the king's messengers, Rahab told the spies:

I know that the Lord has given you the land, that the terror of you has fallen on us, and that all the inhabitants of the land are fainthearted because of you. For we have heard how the Lord dried up the water of the Red Sea for you when you came out of Egypt, and what you did to the two kings of the Amorites who were on the other side of Jordan, Sihon and Og, whom you utterly destroyed. And as soon as we heard these things, our hearts melted; neither did there remain any more courage in anyone because of you, for the Lord your God, He is God in heaven above and on earth beneath. Now therefore, I beg you, swear to me by the Lord, since I have shown you kindness, that you also will show kindness to my father's house, and give me a true token, and spare my father, my mother, my brothers, my sisters, and all that they have, and deliver our lives from death (Joshua 2:9-13 NKJV).*

Now remember that Rahab was a harlot, a prostitute. This was about as low as one could sink in Bible times. Think about what her home life must have been like. Talk about dysfunctional. Men were coming and going at all hours of the day and night. In addition, she and her family lived in an idolatrous, sinful city that was coming under God's judgment. Here was a woman with a tragic past, a dismal present and—in the natural—no future to look forward to. No chance for a new beginning.

That is until the day the two spies came calling. Rahab hid these men of God, lied to protect them, and then she told them that she had heard of their previous victories over the Amorites, Sihon, and Og. She informed them that *"...as soon as we heard these things, our hearts melted; neither did there remain any more courage in anyone because of you."* Then she boldly declared: *"...for the Lord your God, He is God in heaven above and on earth beneath."*

Rahab was on the road to a new beginning. She embraced the Lord as the one true God of Heaven and earth. In this proclamation acknowledging His Lordship, she was in essence saying, He is greater than my past and my present. He is greater than my sin and shame.

That is the starting point to change the future for your own family. Acknowledge that God is the Lord of your dysfunctional home. He is greater than your fractured family. He is greater than your mate's obstinacy to the Gospel. God is more powerful than the addiction of your children. He is greater than their rebellion. *"...for the Lord your God, He is God in heaven above and on earth beneath."* He is greater than the anger, resentment, and hostilities existing in your home. He is God of Heaven and earth and God of your family. Make this declaration today: *He is greater!*

ON THE WAY TO A NEW FUTURE

Rahab boldly asked the spies to spare her life and her family when Israel invaded Jericho. The two spies agreed to this request and Rahab helped them escape over the city wall from a window in her home.

The spies told Rahab to hang a scarlet cord from the window through which they escaped so they could easily identify her house and spare her and her family when Israel invaded:

> *Behold, when we come into the land, thou shalt bind this line of scarlet thread in the window which thou didst let us down by: and thou shalt bring thy father, and thy mother, and thy brethren, and all thy father's household, home unto thee. And it shall be, that whosoever shall go out of the doors of thy house into the street, his blood shall be upon his head, and we will be guiltless: and whosoever shall be with thee in the house, his blood shall be on our head, if any hand be upon him. And she said, According unto your words, so be it. And she sent them away, and they departed: and she bound the scarlet line in the window* (Joshua 2:18-19,21).

The scarlet cord from Rahab's window was a symbol of redemption through the blood and faith in the promise of God: *"...when I see the blood, I will pass over you..."* (Exod. 12:13). This covenant was established by God

72

when Israel was delivered from Egypt. A lamb was sacrificed by each family, and its blood placed on the door posts of the home. When God's judgment fell, each home marked by the blood was excluded.

The Israelites were saved by the blood. The scarlet cord hung from Rahab's window was symbolic of her declaration of faith in the blood, and her family was spared. Your family will be saved in the same way—through application of the blood of Jesus.

Have you prayed for years for your loved ones, without visible results? Are you interceding for a lost son or daughter, parent, or spouse? Don't give up! Don't back down. Each time you pray for their salvation or their deliverance, you are spiritually placing the scarlet thread of the blood of Jesus Christ over them.

Keep pleading that precious blood of Jesus over your family. The blood is just as powerful as in the day of Israel's deliverance. It is just as powerful to deliver as when Rahab hung the scarlet cord from the window of her home. God sees the blood of His Lamb, the Lord Jesus Christ.

THE SHAKING HAS STARTED

Having eluded the enemy, the spies returned from Jericho and declared to Joshua:

> *Truly the Lord has delivered all the land into our hands, for indeed all the inhabitants of the country are fainthearted because of us* (Joshua 2:24).

A few days later, the Jordan River parted, and the Israelites walked across on dry ground. The people of Jericho peered across their walls to see a crowd of Israelites walking around the city in a silent procession. For six days, the strange ritual was repeated. On the seventh day, the people walked silently around the city again but this time at the conclusion of their walk seven priests with trumpets blew their horns. The people began to shout, and the earth trembled. Foundations cracked. The walls (which had safeguarded the city for years) collapsed.

Do you remember where Rahab's house was? It was built on the walls. It was probably on a wooden foundation stretching between them, according to archeological findings. What tremendous faith this woman demonstrated to remain in her house while the walls of the city were shaking and crumbling in the dust.

Apostle Paul warns:

> *See that ye refuse not Him that speaketh. For if they escaped not who refused Him that spake on earth, much more shall not we escape, if we turn away from Him that speaketh from heaven: Whose voice then shook the earth: but now He hath promised, saying, Yet once more I shake not the earth only, but also heaven. And this word, Yet once more, signifieth the removing of those things that are shaken, as of things that are made, that those things which cannot be shaken may remain. Wherefore we receiving a kingdom which cannot be moved, let us have grace, whereby we may serve God acceptably with reverence and godly fear* (Hebrews 12:25-28).

God is shaking the foundations of nations, leaders, the Church, the family, and every facet of society. The purpose of this shaking is to remove the things that can be shaken—the temporal, fleshly, sinful things—so that the things that are eternal and cannot be shaken will remain.

In the past years, we have seen entire nations crumble. The major Communist bloc dissolved almost overnight. We have seen great political leaders fall and seen national economies shaken. We have seen a major shaking of the Church, with the sins of professing Christian leaders being exposed.

The purpose? So that they who could not be shaken, who built their spiritual house on the true foundation of Jesus Christ, could stand. The shaking is enabling the Kingdom of God, which cannot be moved, to be established.

If you and your family are to embrace a new future, then you must experience a shaking. Things must change so that a new foundation can be established in your family. As Israel was the instrument through which God manifested the shaking in Jericho, you must step boldly forward to be used of God in the shaking that needs to occur in your family.

Don't just sit back and let the sin and dysfunction continue. Don't overlook the rebellion. Boldly declare Jesus as Lord of your home, and then begin to shake things up by instituting changes as He directs you.

Clean house spiritually. You might need to do it materially also. You may need to throw out ungodly music, books, movies, and games. In prayer, bind the spirits of addiction, friction, abuse, and dysfunction that are destroying your family. Call a family meeting and declare that these things will no longer be allowed in your home.

Ask God for a plan to change things for your family. He will give you direction, just as He did for Rahab the harlot.

HOUSEHOLD SALVATION

The walls were shaking and crumbling all around, but there they stayed. Rahab and her entire family were rescued because from the window of their home fluttered the scarlet cord. You, too, must place the blood of Jesus over your household and then stand your ground. Don't back down. Don't let the enemy run rampant in your home.

Then Joshua said to the two men who had spied out the country:

> ..."Go into the harlot's house, and from there bring out the woman and all that she has, as you swore to her." And the young men who had been spies went in and brought out Rahab, her father, her mother, her brothers, and all that she had. So they brought out all her relatives and left them outside the camp of Israel (Joshua 6:22-23 NKJV).

This example is a great spiritual parallel of household salvation. Rahab interceded for her family. She instituted a God-directed plan for change, and her entire family was saved.

Biblical records also reveal that this woman later became the wife of Salmon, a prince of Judah. She gave birth to Boaz who married Ruth, who bore a son named Obed. Obed was the father of Jesse, who was the father of King David, through whose line came Jesus Christ. Rahab is listed among the ancestors of the Lord in Matthew 1:5.

James commended Rahab for the faith that was demonstrated by her works. (Read James 2:25.) The writer of Hebrews enrolled her in the hall of fame of the faith-filled. He declared:

> By faith the harlot Rahab did not perish with those who did not believe, when she had received the spies with peace (Hebrews 11:31 NKJV).

Talk about a new future for a family! From the life of a prostitute to an ancestor of the Lord, Jesus Christ! Enrolled in the hall of fame of the faithful!

THE PHILIPPIAN JAILER'S HOUSEHOLD

The story of Rahab is not the only example of household salvation in the Bible. In Acts chapter 16, we find that Paul and Silas were incarcerated for preaching the proof-producing Gospel in the city of Philippi. The masters of a demon-possessed girl were angered by her deliverance because they couldn't make money from her fortune-telling anymore. They fabricated lies against Paul and Silas and:

> ...the multitude rose up together against them: and the magistrates rent off their clothes, and commanded to beat them. And when they had laid many stripes upon them, they cast them into prison, charging the jailor to keep them safely: Who, having received such a charge, thrust them into the inner prison, and made their feet fast in the stocks. And at midnight Paul and Silas prayed, and sang praises unto God: and the prisoners heard them. And suddenly there was a great earthquake, so that the foundations of the prison were shaken: and immediately all the doors were opened, and every one's bands

were loosed. And the keeper of the prison awaking out of his sleep, and seeing the prison doors open, he drew out his sword, and would have killed himself, supposing that the prisoners had been fled. But Paul cried with a loud voice, saying, Do thyself no harm: for we are all here (Acts 16:22-28).

In response to the praises of His servants, God moved in a miraculous demonstration of power. He sent an earthquake that shook the foundations of the prison, the doors were opened, and the bands securing the prisoners loosed. That is what the shaking does. It shakes old foundations, opens doors to a new future, and looses the bonds that have kept you captive.

The Philippian jailer—fearing that the prisoners had escaped, that he would be shamed for dereliction of duty, and that he most likely would pay for it with his life—was ready to kill himself. Paul cried out: *"...Do thyself no harm: for we are all here."*

Then the jailer *"...called for a light, and sprang in, and came trembling, and fell down before Paul and Silas"* (Acts 16:29). He brought Paul and Silas out of the dungeon and asked them: *"...Sirs, what must I do to be saved?"* (Acts 16:30).

Paul and Silas replied:

...Believe on the Lord Jesus Christ, and thou shalt be saved, and thy house. And they spake unto him the word of the Lord, and to all that were in his house. And he took them the same hour of the night, and washed their stripes; and was baptized, he and all his, straightway. And when he had brought them into his house, he set meat before them, and rejoiced, believing in God with all his house (Acts 16:31-34).

The jailer took Paul and Silas at their word. He let them share the Gospel with his entire household and that same night he and his family were baptized: *"...believing in God with all his house"* (Acts 16:34).

This is one of the greatest promises of household salvation in the Word of God: *"...Believe on the Lord Jesus Christ, and thou shalt be saved, and thy house"* (Acts 16:31). Start claiming this promise for your household every day. Come against the sin, rebellion, and dysfunction of your fractured family. Proclaim God's covenant of household salvation.

You may be thinking right now, *I've already prayed this and nothing happened.* Don't give up. Keep holding on to the promise. Keep claiming it. Abraham, Moses, and many others in the Bible had to wait some time before the promises of God were manifested in their lives.

It all comes down to this: Do you believe God's Word or not? God's Word says: *"...Believe on the Lord Jesus Christ, and thou shalt be saved, and thy house"* (Acts 16:31). That is what God says. The question is, what will you say? Will you accept His promise and declare it over your household?

Stop speaking words of defeat and despair over your household. Begin to speak words of faith. Your words are powerful. Be careful what you speak over your family. The Bible declares: *"Death and life are in the power of the tongue..."* (Prov. 18:21). Speak words of life. Make this declaration over your family every day: *I believe in the Lord Jesus Christ. I am saved, and my household will be saved!*

THE HOUSEHOLD OF CORNELIUS

Another tremendous account of a family being set on the road to a new future is found in Acts chapters 10-11, in the story of a man named Cornelius. The Bible records that Cornelius was *"...a devout man, and one that feared God with all his house, which gave much almost to the people, and prayed to God always"* (Acts 10:1-2). He was a good man, a religious man, but he wasn't a saved man.

One day, as Cornelius was praying, God directed him to send men to the apostle Peter and ask him to come and *"...tell thee words, whereby thou and all thy house shall be saved"* (Acts 11:14).

Meanwhile, God gave Peter a vision to prepare him for the arrival of Cornelius' servants. (Read Acts 10:9-17.) Peter accompanied them back to where Cornelius lived. *"And the morrow after they entered into Caesarea. And Cornelius waited for them, and had called together his kinsmen and near friends"* (Acts 10:24). Peter preached the Gospel to them, and *"While Peter* yet spake these words, the Holy Ghost fell on all them which heard the word"* (Acts 10:44). Cornelius and his entire household were saved and baptized that day. Their lives were changed, and the entire family was set on the road to a new future.

RESTORING FRACTURED FAMILIES

Here are five important keys for preventing problems or restoring a fractured family.

1. Establish God and His Word as the Final Authority in Your Home

Give God and His Word priority in your home. Read a few verses over your children every day before they leave the house. Institute family devotions. God told Joshua,

> *Do not let this Book of the Law depart from your mouth; meditate on it day and night, so that you may be careful to do everything written in it. Then you will be prosperous and successful. Have I not commanded you? Be strong and courageous. Do not be terrified; do not be discouraged, for the Lord your God will be with you wherever you go* (Joshua 1:8-9 NIV).

Only a home built on the foundation of God's Word will stand the storms, trials, and tests of life. Jesus said:

> *Therefore everyone who hears these words of mine and puts them into practice is like a wise man who built his house on the rock. The rain came down, the streams rose, and the winds blew and beat against that house; yet it did not fall, because it had its foundation on the rock. But everyone who hears these words of mine and does not put them into practice is like a foolish man who built his house on sand. The rain came down, the streams rose, and the winds blew*

and beat against that house, and it fell with a great crash
(Matthew 7:24-27 NIV).

The psalmist declared: *"Except the Lord build the house, they labour in vain that build it..."* (Ps. 127:1).

If you are a parent, it is your responsibility to establish the Word in your home:

> *And these words, which I command thee this day, shall be in thine heart: And thou shalt teach them diligently unto thy children, and shalt talk of them when thou sittest in thine house, and when thou walkest by the way, and when thou liest down, and when thou risest up* (Deuteronomy 6:6-7).

Don't let the rolling eyes and sighs of that rebellious teenager keep you from establishing the Word in your home. Despite his negative, outward response, his spirit is being affected by the Word. God has promised that it will ultimately bring change:

> *So shall my word be that goeth forth out of my mouth: it shall not return unto me void, but it shall accomplish that which I please, and it shall prosper in the thing whereto I sent it* (Isaiah 55:11).

If you haven't been giving the Word of God priority in your home, begin right now, today. The final authority in every disagreement, every issue, and every question in your home should be the Word of God.

2. Set Godly Standards

By establishing the Word of God as the priority in your home, you will be able to set godly standards. Let your children know that just because everybody else is doing it doesn't mean your family will do it.

Don't allow sinful movies, music, publications, or video games in your home. When you do, you are giving a foothold to the enemy. *"Neither give place to the devil"* (Eph. 4:27). Don't leave room for satan in your home!

Establish godly standards of conduct toward one another. Don't allow anger and disrespect. Set standards for your children's associates. The Bible warns: *"Make no friendship with an angry man; and with a furious man thou shalt not go: Lest thou learn his ways, and get a snare to thy soul"* (Prov. 22:24-25). If you allow your children to hang out with rebellious kids, they will become rebellious. If they run with angry kids, they will soon develop an angry spirit. The friendships your child develops will either be blessings or snares to their souls.

3. Establish Biblical Structure

Paul's instruction regarding structure was given for a Christian home where the father loves the wife as Christ loves the Church. It is not applicable in ungodly homes where the man is abusive and where immoral and ungodly conduct occurs.

In a Christian home, where the father loves his wife as Christ loved the Church, the man is to be the head of the home, the wife should honor his leadership, and the children should obey their parents. (Read Ephesians 5:22-33 and 6:1.) Submission in the Christian home is to be to one another, in the fear of God. (Read Ephesians 5:21.)

The Bible states that rebellion is as the sin of witchcraft. (Read First Samuel 15:22-23.) Wives, if you are in rebellion against your godly husband or allow your children to be rebellious, you are allowing witchcraft into your home!

> *Let all bitterness, and wrath, and anger, and clamour, and evil speaking, be put away from you, with all malice: And be ye kind one to another, tenderhearted, forgiving one another, even as God for Christ's sake hath forgiven you* (Ephesians 4:31-32).

Husbands, if you do not love your wife as Christ loved the Church—being willing to die for Her—then you cannot be the leader God intends in your home.

4. Set a Guard Against Enemy Attacks

Be assured, satan will launch attacks against your home. The home is one of his major targets, as it is the foundation of the Church and society. Like Nehemiah did in Old Testament times, set a watch against the enemy. Be alert for enemy attacks and resist the enemy using your spiritual weapons:

> Be sober, be vigilant; because your adversary the devil, as a roaring lion, walketh about, seeking whom he may devour: Whom resist stedfast in the faith, knowing that the same afflictions are accomplished in your brethren that are in the world (1 Peter 5:8-9).

Don't give satan a foothold in your family. Resist him with the same passion as you would resist a home invasion or a dangerous intruder.

5. Refuse to Let Anything Destroy Your Unity

At the tower of Babel, God declared that nothing would be impossible to the people because of their unity. Finances, sex, in-laws, and problems with your children all have the capacity to destroy unity in your home. Don't allow it.

Gather the family around you, even if they are resistant. Admit the disunity. Ask God's forgiveness. Commit your entire family to unity. Unity is a spirit. Disunity is a spirit. Bind the spirit of disunity, and release the spirit of unity:

> May the God who gives endurance and encouragement give you a spirit of unity among yourselves as you follow Christ Jesus (Romans 15:5 NIV).

Unity does not mean that you will all agree on every little question and issue that arises in your household. Honest, respectful discussion of varying opinions is good to clarify issues and arrive at wholesome decisions. What you want to guard against is allowing different opinions to create disunity, hostility, anger, and unforgiveness. Apostle Paul declared:

I appeal to you, brothers, in the name of our Lord Jesus Christ, that all of you agree with one another so that there may be no divisions among you and that you may be perfectly united in mind and thought (1 Corinthians 1:10 NIV).

Unity takes effort. The Word declares: *"Make every effort to keep the unity of the Spirit through the bond of peace"* (Eph. 4:3 NIV).

Many of us are praying, *Oh, Lord, bless me.* We seek the blessings of God and do not understand why we sometimes fail to receive. If you are not in unity in your home, then you are not in a place where God can bless you.

Psalm 133:1 (NIV) declares: *"How good and pleasant it is when brothers live together in unity."* This verse not only applies to brothers and sisters in the Church, it goes for moms and dads, children, grandchildren, and in-laws too!

Not only is it good and pleasant to live together in unity, it is *"...there the Lord commanded the blessing, even life for evermore"* (Ps. 133:3). God wants your family to function in unity because it is good and pleasant, and it also enables Him to command His blessings upon you.

If you want your home blessed, come into unity. When you are in unity, you won't have to seek God's blessing upon your family. He has already commanded it!

A NEW FUTURE FOR YOUR FAMILY

Restoration is possible for your fractured family. We have seen it in the stories and promises we studied in this chapter.

Your home is not unique with its problems. Every home is dysfunctional to some extent, because every home is affected by sin, no matter how nice the neighborhood or how good the environment. Adam and Eve had a perfect environment, yet dysfunction occurred because of their sin and fear, shame, and blame resulted.

Abraham had a fractured family with disharmony between his sons, Isaac and Ishmael, and their mothers. Esau and Jacob experienced sibling rivalry from the womb. Jacob had two wives in the home, each conspiring one against the other.

Yet from these fractured families, God raised up powerful men and women to accomplish His purposes. Abraham became the father of nations. Joseph came from Jacob's dysfunctional home, and saved a nation from famine. And, as we learned, Rahab became an ancestor of Jesus Christ, and the families of Cornelius and the Philippian jailer were set on the road to new destinies.

God wants to do the same for your family. Don't give up. Don't lose hope. Your family can have a new beginning. Embrace the promises of household salvation we studied in this chapter. Intercede for your family. Institute positive, biblical changes. In so doing, you will assure a new future for your family.

Sometimes, problems in families are due to deep emotional wounds experienced by an individual. In the next chapter, you will learn how to recover from these and experience a new beginning emotionally.

CHAPTER 8

RECOVERING FROM EMOTIONAL WOUNDS

God wants to heal you from the emotional wounds of your past. You may be engulfed with grief for a loved one who has died, hurting from divorce, or suffering emotional scars from being rejected, abused, or abandoned. Whatever emotional hurts you have suffered, God wants you to recover. He wants to give you a new beginning in the emotional realm.

There are many ways we experience emotional wounds, but most of these can be categorized into one of five areas as illustrated by the following biblical examples:

1. Emotional Wounds Result From the Actions of Others

Joseph is a good example. Through no fault of his own, Joseph was sold into Egypt by his brothers, imprisoned falsely because of the accusations of Potiphar's wife, and forgotten by those he helped in prison. The actions of other people around him resulted in deep emotional wounds.

Joseph's hurt is evident in his comment: *"For indeed I was stolen away out of the land of the Hebrews: and here also have I done nothing that they should put me into the dungeon"* (Gen. 40:15).

We live in a sinful world and you most likely won't make it through this life without being emotionally wounded by others. But listen to Joseph's final analysis. In the end, he declared:

Now therefore be not grieved, nor angry with yourselves, that
ye sold me hither; for God did send me before you to preserve
life. So now it was not you that sent me hither but God...
(Genesis 45:5,8).

God is at work, even in the emotional wounds inflicted on you by
others. His specialty is taking what is intended for evil and turning it to
good. Joseph declared: *"But as for you, ye thought evil against me; but God*
meant it unto good, to bring to pass, as it is this day, to save much people alive"
(Gen. 50:20).

You may have been wounded by others in the past, but it doesn't have to
abort your future. If you let Him, God will turn what was intended for evil
for your good and use it to propel you into your destiny.

2. *Emotional Wounds Result From the Circumstances of Life*

This is illustrated by the experiences of Naomi recorded in the Book
of Ruth. Naomi went through a famine, had to leave her home, and
experienced the death of her husband and sons and abandonment by a
daughter-in-law.

Until Jesus returns, we all will experience wounds through circumstances
of life. For example, until Christ returns and the final enemy of death is conquered, we all will face death. Death entered this world through the original
sin of man and it is a circumstance that we all will encounter, for *"...it is*
appointed unto man once to die..." (Heb. 9:27).

After Naomi experienced these tragic circumstances of life, she said, No
longer call me *Naomi* (which means "pleasant" and "blessed"), but call me
Mara. The name *Mara* means "bitter." Naomi had grown bitter and disillusioned by the emotional wounds that she had incurred.

Later on, however, after a miraculous restoration, Naomi recovered from
her emotional wounds, was reinstated as part of a happy family unit, and
became an ancestor of the Lord, Jesus Christ.

You will experience difficult circumstances in life that will wound
you emotionally. The question is, will you let them make you bitter
or better?

3. *Emotional Wounds Result From Ministry for the Lord*

The New Testament speaks of suffering for His name's sake (Acts 9:16), on behalf of Christ (Phil. 1:29), for the Kingdom of God (2 Thess. 1:5), for the Gospel (2 Tim. 1:11-12), for well-doing (1 Peter 2:19-20; 3:17), for righteousness' sake (1 Pet. 3:14), for being a Christian (1 Pet. 4:15-16), and according to the will of God (1 Pet. 4:19).

Apostle Paul said that while on a mission in Asia he was so utterly crushed that he despaired of life itself. (Read Second Corinthians 1:8.) He presents a different image from that of the cheerful evangelist who promises believers nothing but peace and prosperity. When Paul was first called by God to ministry, he would suffer for the sake of the Lord. (Read Acts 9:16.) Paul's response to this suffering was to endure the loss of all things to win some for Christ. He told believers *"For it has been granted to you on behalf of Christ not only to believe, but to suffer for Him"* (Phil. 1:29 NIV).

Paul was not alone in suffering for ministry. The whole Church suffered in New Testament times. Hebrews chapter 11 records the stories of some of the cruel persecutions that they endured. Many of these men and women of faith were delivered by the power of God. Prison doors opened and they walked out. Some were sentenced to death in fiery furnaces, but emerged unaffected by the flames.

Some of these believers, however (who are also called *men and women of faith*) did not receive deliverance. They were imprisoned, afflicted, tormented, and even martyred because of their testimony of the Gospel. (Read Hebrews 11:36-40.) Talk about emotional wounds! These people certainly had justification to harbor them!

We focus on living faith, but God also reveals His power in dying faith. This is the faith that is manifested in difficult times, not just in good times when a mighty deliverance is manifested.

Sometimes you will not understand the sorrows and difficulties you experience, but the Bible says to commit these things to the Lord.

Yet if any man suffer as a Christian let him not be ashamed;
but let him glorify God on this behalf. Wherefore let them

*that suffer according to the will of God commit the keeping
of their souls to him in well doing, as unto a faithful Creator*
(1 Peter 4:16,19).

4. *Emotional Wounds Result From Direct satanic Activity*

This is evident in the story of Job. God's testimony of Job was that he was a righteous man. (Read Job chapters 1-2.) Job did not suffer because he had sinned, as his friends claimed. They believed if Job repented, his circumstances would change. Job did not suffer because of anything he had done. Job was a righteous man. This was God's testimony of Job, Job's testimony of himself, and his reputation before man.

There are two important truths revealed by Job's suffering. The first is that behind every circumstance of life there is a spiritual cause. In the natural world, we would say it was a terrible accident that the roof fell in and killed Job's children. We might blame the Chaldean forces for seizing his herds and attribute his skin infection to allergies or a virus. But there are no accidents in the lives of believers. Our world is not out of control. God is the sovereign Lord over every circumstance.

Behind the scenes in the spiritual world was the true cause of Job's problems. There was a spiritual battle going on over his heart, mind, and allegiance. It was also a battle between the forces of Heaven and hell.

There is a warfare going on in the spiritual world over you and it is manifested in the difficult circumstances you experience in the natural world. Behind every natural circumstance you are facing there is a spiritual cause.

The second important truth evident in Job's suffering is that nothing can enter the life of a believer without God's knowledge. God does not cause our suffering. It is inflicted by satan, but its limits are set by God.

Job was a wealthy man with many blessings, but he lost it all during this spiritual battle. Sometimes all that a man has is in the hands of satan. The question is, can you serve God on the basis of who He is and not what you receive from Him? Will you still serve God if there are no benefits attached? Will you serve God simply because He is God? Will you lay aside your unexplained losses and remain faithful?

5. *Emotional Wounds Result From Our Own Sin*

Jonah is a good example of this. In disobedience to God, Jonah headed the opposite direction from Nineveh where he had been commanded to go and preach repentance. He experienced a terrible storm at sea and ended up in the belly of a great fish because of his own sin. (Read Jonah chapters 1-2.)

These five basic categories encompass areas in which we commonly experience emotional wounds. Now let us establish this principle right up front: There is only one solution for the emotional wounds caused by your own sin, and that is repentance. Only when Jonah repented was he delivered. (Read Jonah chapter 3.)

What about the emotional wounds caused through no fault of your own? What is your response to hurts caused by others, because of your ministry, through the natural circumstances of life, or due to direct satanic attacks? How do you respond to these hurts for which you are not responsible, for which you can see no visible meaning and purpose?

WRONG RESPONSES TO EMOTIONAL WOUNDS

It takes both positive and negative to produce power. If we are to have power to recover from our emotional wounds, then we must first eliminate the wrong ways we have responded to them.

We Murmur and Complain

Complaining is different from honest questioning. All murmuring is actually against God who is taking all the circumstances of our lives, both bad and good, and using them to accomplish His purpose:

> *And we know that all things work together for good to them that love God, to them who are the called according to His purpose. For whom He did foreknow, He also did predestinate to be conformed to the image of His Son, that He might be the firstborn among many brethren* (Romans 8:28-29).

God is using every circumstance of life to conform you to His image. It is the enemy who comes to kill, steal, and destroy, but God uses what is intended for evil and turns it for your good. When you complain against any of these things (even the emotional wounds you experience), you are in reality complaining against God and His work in your life. If you have been murmuring and complaining about your emotional hurts, stop right now and ask God to forgive you.

We Develop a Vindictive, Bitter, Angry Spirit

When the warriors of Israel lost a great battle, they wanted to take revenge on David. They talked of stoning him because the enemy had defeated them and taken their possessions. (Read First Samuel 30:6.) They were emotionally wounded, but responded improperly to their losses.

The Bible uses the wormwood plant as the symbol of bitterness. In the natural world, the liquor made from this plant leads to mental deterioration and death. The same is true in the spiritual world. Deuteronomy 29:18 cautions against the spiritual root that bears gall and wormwood.

Apostle Paul warned: *"Looking diligently lest any man fail of the grace of God; lest any root of bitterness springing up trouble you, and thereby many be defiled"* (Heb. 12:15).

Peter told Simeon he was in the gall of bitterness. (Read Acts 8:23.) *Gall* means "poison." Bitterness will poison you and those around you. If you have a vindictive, bitter, angry spirit, ask God to forgive you. Ask Him to dig out the root of bitterness from your life.

We Become Depressed and Discouraged

Jeremiah wrote of such a response when he said:

> ...My strength and my hope is perished from the Lord; remembering mine affliction and my misery, the wormwood and the gall. My soul hath them still in remembrance, and is humbled in me (Lamentations 3:18-20).

Any time you get your focus on the hurts you have experienced, you will become depressed and discouraged. Change your focus from your hurts to the Healer.

We Refuse to Forgive

One of the most common responses to emotional wounds is unforgiveness. Someone hurts, abuses, or abandons us, and we refuse to forgive.

True forgiveness comes by recognizing what was done to you was wrong, the result of sinful men in a sinful world. Acknowledge what happened and how it affected you, then confess your hurt to God and ask Him to heal your emotions. You may not ever forget the *fact* of the incident, but what you are in need of is healing from the *pain* of it.

Ask God to help you forgive others involved, then by an act of your will, forgive them even as Christ forgives you. Recognize that God extends forgiveness to you as you forgive others. Part of the daily prayer Christ gave us is…*forgive us our trespasses, as we forgive those who trespass against us.*

When you forgive, you are not freeing the person who hurt you of personal responsibility for his or her actions. You are setting yourself free to be healed of your emotional wounds.

GOD WORKS THROUGH EMOTIONAL WOUNDS

If you are a person of faith, there are positive things that happen spiritually if you can learn to respond properly to emotional hurts. Let's look at a few of them.

Your Faith Is Tested

Everything in the spiritual world is based on faith. This is why the strength of your faith must be tested:

> *That the trial of your faith being much more precious than of gold that perisheth though it be tried with fire, might be found unto praise and honour and glory at the appearing of Jesus Christ* (1 Peter 1:7).

You Learn How to Comfort Others

Paul wrote:

Blessed be God, even the Father of our Lord Jesus Christ, the Father of mercies, and the God of all comfort; Who comforteth us in all our tribulation that we may be able to comfort them which are in any trouble, by the comfort wherewith we ourselves are comforted of God (2 Corinthians 1:3-4).

When you experience suffering and learn to properly respond to emotional wounds, you can help others who face similar difficulties.

You Learn Not to Trust Your Own Natural Resources

Paul wrote of his sufferings in Asia:

...in Asia, that we were pressed out of measure, above strength, insomuch that we despaired even of life: But we had the sentence of death in ourselves, that we should not trust in ourselves, but in God which raiseth the dead: (2 Corinthians 1:8-9).

The reason Paul went through this was *"...that the excellency of the power may be of God, and not of us"* (2 Cor. 4:7).

You Develop Positive Spiritual Qualities

When you deal with emotional wounds properly, you will develop positive spiritual qualities in your life.

We glory in tribulations also: knowing that tribulation worketh patience; and patience, experience; and experience, hope: And hope maketh not ashamed; because the love of God is shed abroad in our hearts... (Romans 5:3-5).

...after that ye have suffered awhile, make you perfect, stablish, strengthen, settle you (1 Peter 5:10).

These qualities conform you to the image of Jesus, which is God's plan for you. (Read Romans 8:28-29.)

God's Power Is Perfected

God told Paul: *"...My grace is sufficient for thee; for my strength is made perfect in weakness..."* (2 Cor. 12:9). Paul responded: *"Most gladly therefore will I rather glory in my infirmities, that the power of Christ may rest upon me"* (2 Cor. 12:9). It is in your weakness—your emotional wounds and hurts—that God's power is perfected.

Your Focus Is Changed From Temporal to Eternal

God wants to change your focus from the emotional wounds to their eternal benefits. Paul declared:

> *For our light affliction, which is but for a moment, worketh for us a far more exceeding and eternal weight of glory; While we look not at the things which are seen, but at the things which are not seen; for the things which are seen are temporal; but the things which are not seen are eternal* (2 Corinthians 4:17-18).

God works in your painful issue and uses it only when you are focused on eternal things rather than the problem itself. Trials and problems in life are not unusual or without purpose:

> *Beloved, think it not strange concerning the fiery trial which is to try you, as though some strange thing happened unto you: But rejoice, inasmuch as ye are partakers of Christ's sufferings; that, when His glory shall be revealed, ye may be glad also with exceeding joy* (1 Peter 4:12-13).

You Are Chosen by God

You have asked to be used by God. You desire to be more like Jesus and have prayed to be a chosen vessel for His use. God answers your prayer through difficulties:

> *Behold I have refined thee, but not with silver; I have chosen thee in the furnace of affliction* (Isaiah 48:10).

How will you come out of the furnace of affliction? Chosen or an emotional cripple?

A PROPER RESPONSE TO EMOTIONAL WOUNDS

So what is the proper response to emotional hurts? How can we avoid negative responses and embrace the positive things God wants to do in the midst of our suffering?

To answer these questions, let's examine an event that occurred in the Old Testament. In Exodus chapter 15, we learn that after Israel fled Egypt and went into the wilderness, they were badly in need of water. Moses took their needs to the Lord:

> *...and the Lord shewed him a tree, which when he had cast into the waters, the waters were made sweet; there He made for them a statute and an ordinance, and there He proved them* (Exodus 15:25).

In Isaiah we read:

> *And there shall come forth a rod out of the stem of Jesse, and a branch shall grow out of His roots; And the Spirit of the Lord shall rest upon Him, and the spirit of wisdom and understanding, the spirit of counsel and might, the spirit of knowledge and of the fear of the Lord; And shall make Him of quick understanding in the fear of the Lord; and He shall not judge after the sight of His eyes, neither reprove after the hearing of His ears* (Isaiah 11:1-3).

The emotional wounds of your life (all of the bitterness and hurts) can only be healed when you cast the spiritual branch of the Lord, Jesus Christ, into that situation. The tree on the bank (in Exodus 15) is symbolic of the Cross of Christ and of Jesus Himself.

You will not face your emotional hurts alone. The Bible confirms that *"In all their affliction, He was afflicted..."* (Isa. 63:9). There is a healing branch on the bank. It is the Lord, Jesus Christ.

God did not cause your hurts, but He will redeem them. To *redeem* something means "to buy up of each opportunity and turn it to the best advantage." What the world views as an ordeal, God views as an opportunity. The real test of your spiritual maturity is how you respond in the day of distress: *"If thou faint in the day of adversity, thy strength is small"* (Prov. 24:10).

Jesus understood emotional pain. He sighed, which is one of the most significant tokens of excessive grief (see Mark 8:12). He wept (see John 11:35). He sweat great drops of blood in the Garden of Gethsemane prior to His death (see Luke 22:44). Jesus didn't remain in a chronic condition of emotional trauma. Each time He experienced the hurts of life, there arose within Him a simultaneous faith that God was sufficient for His suffering.

Jesus is sufficient for your pain. He will heal every emotional wound and set you on the pathway to a new beginning. Release your hurts to Him right now. Release all the pain and shame of your past. Forgive those who caused your pain. Then raise your hands, and praise God for healing your emotional wounds.

Now you are ready to experience supernatural abundance. You will learn how in Chapter 9.

CHAPTER 9

EXPERIENCING SUPERABUNDANCE

Credit card debt. Threats of foreclosure. Bankruptcy. Struggling to make ends meet. Barely surviving from paycheck to paycheck.

God never intended you to live this way. The good news is that you can have a new beginning in your finances—no matter how deeply in debt you may be, no matter what your educational level or job prospects, no matter what kind of financial ruin you may be facing.

If you receive and act on the revelation in this chapter, you can have a new beginning in your finances.

BREAKING THE SPIRIT OF FEAR

One of the first things that attacks your mind when you face financial famine is a spirit of fear. When unexpected emergencies arise (car repairs, doctor and hospital bills, or a delinquent mortgage), fear gets a stranglehold on your mind. You may worry that you will lose your home. You may fret over bills. You may fear that you will never get out from under the debt you have incurred. If you are to have a new beginning in your finances, then you must break the spirit of fear that is operating in your life.

In First Kings chapter 17, there is a tremendous example of a widow who broke through the spirit of fear, acted on the word that was spoken by the prophet Elijah, and received God's supernatural provision into her dire circumstances.

At the time of this account, there was a great famine throughout the land, a famine God had sent in judgment of sin and apostasy. The heavens were shut up and there was no rain, according to the Word of the Lord spoken by Elijah who had prophesied a 3½-year drought. The land became barren and parched, and the crops withered in the fields.

Elijah was in seclusion for some time by the brook Cherith, but there came a day when the brook dried up. Then the Word of the Lord came to him saying: *"Arise, get thee to Zarephath, which belongeth to Zidon, and dwell there: behold, I have commanded a widow woman there to sustain thee"* (1 Kings 17:9).

Now Elijah had already learned one of the key principles of financial provision—to be in God's place at God's time. At Cherith, God had provided for him through both natural means (the brook) and supernatural means (the ravens).

In Bible times, ravens were regarded as omens of misfortune, death, or tragedy and were unclean because of their scavenger habits. God chose unclean birds to feed His prophet! God will provide for you, but it may not be according to your preconceived ideas. Sometimes God provides through natural means, sometimes through the supernatural, but you can be assured that: *"...my God shall supply all your need according to His riches in glory by Christ Jesus"* (Phil. 4:19).

At the Word of the Lord to leave Cherith, Elijah obeyed and went to Zarephath:

> *So he arose and went to Zarephath. And when he came to the gate of the city, behold, the widow woman was there gathering of sticks: and he called to her, and said, Fetch me, I pray thee, a little water in a vessel, that I may drink. And as she was going to fetch it, he called to her, and said, Bring me, I pray thee, a morsel of bread in thine hand. And she said, As the Lord thy God liveth, I have not a cake, but an handful of meal in a barrel, and a little oil in a cruse: and, behold, I am*

gathering two sticks, that I may go in and dress it for me and my son, that we may eat it, and die. And Elijah said unto her, Fear not; go and do as thou hast said: but make me thereof a little cake first, and bring it unto me, and after make for thee and for thy son. For thus saith the Lord God of Israel, The barrel of meal shall not waste, neither shall the cruse of oil fail, until the day that the Lord sendeth rain upon the earth. And she went and did according to the saying of Elijah: and she, and he, and her house, did eat many days. And the barrel of meal wasted not, neither did the cruse of oil fail, according to the word of the Lord, which he spake by Elijah (1 Kings 17:10-16).

When you face financial crises, it is crucial for you to hear the Word of the Lord concerning your circumstances and to act in obedience on what He directs you to do. When God directed Elijah to go to Zarepath, he immediately started on the way.

To demonstrate His supernatural provision for Elijah, God did not choose a rich widow, who had a large storehouse filled with ample provisions. He chose a poor widow woman.

This widow was a Gentile living in a country where the people served Baal. She did not know the God of Israel. She and her son were at a point of starvation. She was at the end of her own natural resources, at the point of her greatest need. She was fearful, had lost hope, and was preparing to die. The good news is that this is when God steps in—when you get to the end of your own natural resources.

Elijah asked this woman to bring him some water and a cake to eat. She responded that all she had was a handful of meal, a little oil, that she was preparing it for a final meal for herself and her family, and then they would prepare to die. This woman's natural resources were totally exhausted and a spirit of fear and hopelessness had her bound.

This may be exactly where you are today. Your "handful of flour and oil" may represent your meager paycheck or bank account. As long as you keep your eyes on your own resources, you will be hopeless. The more you look at your financial problems, the more fearful you will become and the more impossible your situation will seem.

The prophet's first words to this widow woman were, "Fear not!" Then he directed her to use the small provisions she had to make a cake and bring it to him first. Then she could make something for herself and her son. Elijah gave her God's promise:

> For thus saith the Lord God of Israel, The barrel of meal shall not waste, neither shall the cruse of oil fail, until the day that the Lord sendeth rain upon the earth (1 Kings 17:14).

This widow received the Word of the Lord and acted on it. She put God first above her own needs. She baked a cake for Elijah first and then she discovered she had enough oil and flour to meet her own needs. As God promised, the jar of flour and the jug of oil did not run dry. Each day, as the widow reached down into the jar for the flour and poured the oil, it multiplied.

What this widow experienced was the supernatural provision of God, a cycle of total provision and continual supply. She learned to depend on the Word of the Lord for daily provision. God did not fill her cupboards with tons of food, although He certainly could have done so. As she looked to God as her source of supernatural supply, He provided for her daily.

God's first Word to you for a new beginning in your finances is: Fear not. In the name of Jesus, break the stronghold of fear from your life. Wait on God until He shows you what to do. Then act on His Word, and believe that He will fulfill it. The same supernatural God who multiplied the flour and oil for the widow will supply what you need. He will multiply what you sow in obedience to His Word. You will have total provision and continual supply as you draw daily from His unlimited resources instead of your own meager fare.

FREED FOR DIVINE PURPOSE

It is time for the Body of Christ to experience a supernatural, spiritual breakthrough in the realm of finances—a new beginning.

God is going to have an end-time people. He will raise them up for a divine purpose, through which He manifests Himself in power. These are people who will join themselves with God in holiness and present their lives as living sacrifices to accomplish God's purpose of reaching the world with the Gospel of Jesus Christ.

It is upon these people that God will release an end-time financial anointing, set them free from indebtedness, and launch them into a divine cycle of supernatural provision. God will do this for divine purpose—the extension of His Kingdom. Jesus said:

> ...Therefore I say unto you, Take no thought for your life, what ye shall eat; neither for the body, what ye shall put on. The life is more than meat, and the body is more than raiment. Consider the ravens: for they neither sow nor reap; which neither have storehouse nor barn; and God feedeth them: how much more are ye better than the fowls? And which of you with taking thought can add to his stature one cubit? If ye then be not able to do that thing which is least, why take ye thought for the rest? Consider the lilies how they grow: they toil not, they spin not; and yet I say unto you, that Solomon in all his glory was not arrayed like one of these. If then God so clothe the grass, which is to day in the field, and to morrow is cast into the oven; how much more will He clothe you, O ye of little faith? And seek not ye what ye shall eat, or what ye shall drink, neither be ye of doubtful mind. For all these things do the nations of the world seek after: and your Father knoweth that ye have need of these things. But rather seek ye the kingdom of God; and all these things shall be added unto you (Luke 12:22-31).

God is raising up a people whose focus will be on the Kingdom of God. They will not worry about what they will eat or drink, what clothing they will put on, or where they will live. They will seek first the Kingdom of God, and all these other things will be given to them.

Let me ask you: Where has your focus been? Has it been on making money, getting ahead materially, and fretting about your debts, or has your focus been on the Kingdom? Believers are called to a divine purpose. When you change your focus from your finances to the divine purpose of extending the Kingdom, you will be amazed at the provision that follows.

SUPERNATURAL DEBT RETIREMENT

Another great Old Testament example illustrates this supernatural financial breakthrough we are talking about:

> *Now there cried a certain woman of the wives of the sons of the prophets unto Elisha, saying, Thy servant my husband is dead; and thou knowest that thy servant did fear the Lord: and the creditor is come to take unto him my two sons to be bondmen. And Elisha said unto her, What shall I do for thee? tell me, what hast thou in the house? And she said, Thine handmaid hath not any thing in the house, save a pot of oil. Then he said, Go, borrow thee vessels abroad of all thy neighbors, even empty vessels; borrow not a few. And when thou art come in, thou shalt shut the door upon thee and upon thy sons, and shalt pour out into all those vessels, and thou shalt set aside that which is full. So she went from him, and shut the door upon her and upon her sons, who brought the vessels to her; and she poured out. And it came to pass, when the vessels were full, that she said unto her son, Bring me yet a vessel. And he said unto her, There is not a vessel more. And the oil stayed. Then she came and told the man of God. And he said, Go, sell the oil, and pay thy debt, and live thou and thy children of the rest (2 Kings 4:1-7).*

In this account, a widow woman faced a desperate situation. Her husband died, and she had no source of income. There was no possible way to meet the needs of her family. She was in debt, and the creditor had come to take her two sons to be slaves for repayment of the debt (a custom at that time).

This woman was desperate. If ever anyone needed a miracle, she did. She had already lost her husband, and now she faced the possibility of losing her sons. In her desperation, she cried out to the prophet Elisha for help. Elisha answered, "What shall I do for you? Tell me, what do you have in the house?" The woman answered that she had nothing except a jar of oil.

Elisha told her to go borrow as many vessels as possible from her neighbors—not a few, but as many as possible. Then she was to go into her house, shut the door, and begin to pour her oil into the vessels she had collected.

The widow acted on the word of the Lord's prophet. She collected the vessels, entered in and shut the door to her house, then took her small bottle of oil and began to pour. As she poured, the oil began to multiply. Can you imagine the amazement she experienced each time she poured the oil and filled another vessel? She kept pouring and pouring until every empty vessel she had collected was filled to the brim. The prophet Elisha then directed her to sell the oil, pay her debt, and free her sons.

Are you ready to act upon the Word of the Lord? Are you a candidate for a miracle of debt cancellation? The key to the miracle of debt cancellation for this widow woman was acting upon the Word of the Lord. God used what she had to give and multiplied it. You may think your finances are so bad that you do not have anything to give. God used a small supply of oil to multiply and meet this woman's great need. Act on God's Word and give what you have, no matter how small it may seem to you.

There is a miracle in your house. It starts with what you have. Your pot of oil may be money, a talent, or an ability that—when sanctified by God—will result in your financial freedom. You may have limited resources, like the little lad in New Testament times, who presented his loaves and fishes to the Master to feed a multitude. Take what little you may have, present it to God, and watch what happens:

> *Give, and it shall be given unto you; good measure, pressed down, and shaken together, and running over, shall men give into your bosom. For with the same measure that ye mete withal it shall be measured to you again* (Luke 6:38).

The flow of oil only stopped when there were no more empty vessels. Begin to pour what you have—your limited financial resources, your talents, your time, and your abilities—into the empty vessels of hurting humanity. As long as you act on the Word, use what you have, and pour your life into empty vessels, your resources will continue to multiply supernaturally.

THE PRINCIPLE OF FIRSTFRUITS

Since we are discussing a new beginning for your finances, reflect on this question. Do you honor God with the firstfruits of your finances? Proverbs 3:9-10 declares: *"Honour the Lord with thy substance, and with the firstfruits of all thine increase: So shall thy barns be filled with plenty, and thy presses shall burst out with new wine."*

What does it mean to honor God with your firstfruits? It means giving to God first. It means paying a tithe of 10 percent of your income. Giving God the firstfruits of your income causes the rest to be blessed. When you honor Him with the firstfruits, He promises that you will have plenty. You will not just have enough to scrape by. You will have plenty!

The Word declares: "If ye be willing and obedient, ye shall eat the good of the land" (Isa. 1:19). If you want to eat of the good of the land and have a new beginning in your finances, then you must be obedient to God's Word. That includes His Word regarding tithes and offerings.

One reason many of God's people are not receiving their financial breakthroughs is their failure in the area of firstfruits. God spoke through the prophet Malachi:

> *Will a man rob God? Yet ye have robbed Me. But ye say, Wherein have we robbed Thee? In tithes and offerings. Ye are cursed with a curse: for ye have robbed Me, even this whole nation. Bring ye all the tithes into the storehouse, that there may be meat in Mine house, and prove Me now herewith, saith the Lord of hosts, if I will not open you the windows of heaven, and pour you out a blessing, that there shall not be room enough to receive it. And I will rebuke the devourer for your sakes, and*

he shall not destroy the fruits of your ground; neither shall your vine cast her fruit before the time in the field, saith the Lord of hosts. And all nations shall call you blessed: for ye shall be a delightsome land, saith the Lord of hosts (Malachi 3:8-12).

When you fail to give God tithes and offerings, you are robbing Him, and your finances are under a curse. When you bring the firstfruits of your tithe to God and faithfully give your offerings, then He opens the windows of Heaven and pours out a blessing that you don't even have room to receive! The devourer—the enemy, who would rob you of finances, health, and happiness if you allowed him to—will be rebuked, and the work of your hands will be blessed.

OBEDIENCE IS THE KEY

There is a powerful Old Testament example that illustrates the truth that obedience is the key. When the people of Israel entered the Promised Land, God gave them some tremendous promises:

Now after the death of Moses the servant of the Lord it came to pass, that the Lord spake unto Joshua the son of Nun, Moses' minister, saying, Moses my servant is dead; now therefore arise, go over this Jordan, thou, and all this people, unto the land which I do give to them, even to the children of Israel. Every place that the sole of your foot shall tread upon, that have I given unto you, as I said unto Moses. From the wilderness and this Lebanon even unto the great river, the river Euphrates, all the land of the Hittites, and unto the great sea toward the going down of the sun, shall be your coast. There shall not any man be able to stand before thee all the days of thy life: as I was with Moses, so I will be with thee: I will not fail thee, nor forsake thee. Be strong and of a good courage: for unto this people shalt thou divide for an inheritance the land, which I sware unto their fathers to give them (Joshua 1:1-6).

God promised His people total victory. Every place that the soles of their feet touched was theirs. No enemy would be able to stand before them and they would inherit the land as God had promised.

There were conditions to these promises:

> *Only be thou strong and very courageous, that thou mayest observe to do according to all the law, which Moses My servant commanded thee: turn not from it to the right hand or to the left, that thou mayest prosper whithersoever thou goest. This book of the law shall not depart out of thy mouth; but thou shalt meditate therein day and night, that thou mayest observe to do according to all that is written therein: for then thou shalt make thy way prosperous, and then thou shalt have good success. Have not I commanded thee? Be strong and of a good courage; be not afraid, neither be thou dismayed: for the Lord thy God is with thee whithersoever thou goest* (Joshua 1:7-9).

Israel must obey God's Word in order to be prosperous, successful, and victorious. Some people are claiming blessings for their finances when they are angry and vindictive, living in unforgiveness and bitterness. Others are addicted, bound by drugs, alcohol, and pornography. Some are having extramarital affairs. You cannot violate God's Word and expect Him to bless your finances. These promises are conditional upon obedience.

When Israel faced their first battle in the Promised Land, God gave them specific instructions concerning the spoil from the city of Jericho, that *"...all the silver, and gold, and vessels of brass and iron, are consecrated unto the Lord: they shall come into the treasury of the Lord"* (Josh. 6:19).

You can read about the battle of Jericho in Joshua chapter 6. God told Joshua:

> *And the Lord said unto Joshua, See, I have given into thine hand Jericho, and the king thereof, and the mighty men of valour. And ye shall compass the city, all ye men of war, and*

go round about the city once. Thus shalt thou do six days.
And seven priests shall bear before the ark seven trumpets of
rams' horns: and the seventh day ye shall compass the city seven
times, and the priests shall blow with the trumpets. And it
shall come to pass, that when they make a long blast with the
ram's horn, and when ye hear the sound of the trumpet, all the
people shall shout with a great shout; and the wall of the city
shall fall down flat, and the people shall ascend up every man
straight before him (Joshua 6:2-5).

A supernatural battle, fought at God's direction, with supernatural
results. There was only one problem:

But the children of Israel committed a trespass in the accursed
thing: for Achan, the son of Carmi, the son of Zabdi, the son
of Zerah, of the tribe of Judah, took of the accursed thing: and
the anger of the Lord was kindled against the children of Israel
(Joshua 7:1).

The full ramifications of this refusal to honor God with the firstfruits of
Jericho emerge in Joshua chapter 7:

And Joshua sent men from Jericho to Ai, which is beside Bethaven,
on the east side of Bethel, and spake unto them, saying, Go up
and view the country. And the men went up and viewed Ai.
And they returned to Joshua, and said unto him, Let not all the
people go up; but let about two or three thousand men go up and
smite Ai; and make not all the people to labour thither; for they
are but few. So there went up thither of the people about three
thousand men: and they fled before the men of Ai. And the men
of Ai smote of them about thirty and six men: for they chased
them from before the gate even unto Shebarim, and smote them
in the going down: wherefore the hearts of the people melted,
and became as water (Joshua 7:2-5).

Ai was a smaller city than Jericho. It should have been easy to conquer. God had promised that no enemy would stand before them. What was wrong?

> *And Joshua rent his clothes, and fell to the earth upon his face before the ark of the Lord until the eventide, he and the elders of Israel, and put dust upon their heads. And Joshua said, Alas, O Lord God, wherefore hast Thou at all brought this people over Jordan, to deliver us into the hand of the Amorites, to destroy us? would to God we had been content, and dwelt on the other side Jordan! O Lord, what shall I say, when Israel turneth their backs before their enemies! For the Canaanites and all the inhabitants of the land shall hear of it, and shall environ us round, and cut off our name from the earth: and what wilt Thou do unto Thy great name? And the Lord said unto Joshua, Get thee up; wherefore liest thou thus upon thy face? Israel hath sinned, and they have also transgressed My covenant which I commanded them: for they have even taken of the accursed thing, and have also stolen, and dissembled also, and they have put it even among their own stuff. Therefore the children of Israel could not stand before their enemies, but turned their backs before their enemies, because they were accursed: neither will I be with you any more, except ye destroy the accursed from among you. Up, sanctify the people, and say, Sanctify yourselves against to morrow: for thus saith the Lord God of Israel, There is an accursed thing in the midst of thee, O Israel: thou canst not stand before thine enemies, until ye take away the accursed thing from among you* (Joshua 7:6-13).

God's people could not stand in victory because they were cursed. They had not obeyed the Word of the Lord with regard to the firstfruits offerings from Jericho. It wasn't until the curse was removed from their midst that God's blessing returned:

And Achan answered Joshua, and said, Indeed I have sinned against the Lord God of Israel, and thus and thus have I done: When I saw among the spoils a goodly Babylonish garment, and two hundred shekels of silver, and a wedge of gold of fifty shekels weight, then I coveted them, and took them; and, behold, they are hid in the earth in the midst of my tent, and the silver under it. So Joshua sent messengers, and they ran unto the tent; and, behold, it was hid in his tent, and the silver under it. And they took them out of the midst of the tent, and brought them unto Joshua, and unto all the children of Israel, and laid them out before the Lord. And Joshua, and all Israel with him, took Achan the son of Zerah, and the silver, and the garment, and the wedge of gold, and his sons, and his daughters, and his oxen, and his asses, and his sheep, and his tent, and all that he had: and they brought them unto the valley of Achor. And Joshua said, Why hast thou troubled us? the Lord shall trouble thee this day. And all Israel stoned him with stones, and burned them with fire, after they had stoned them with stones. And they raised over him a great heap of stones unto this day. So the Lord turned from the fierceness of his anger. Wherefore the name of that place was called, The valley of Achor, unto this day (Joshua 7:20-26).

After Israel repented and eliminated the evil, then God commanded Joshua to return to Ai:

And the Lord said unto Joshua, Fear not, neither be thou dismayed: take all the people of war with thee, and arise, go up to Ai: see, I have given into thy hand the king of Ai, and his people, and his city, and his land: And so it was, that all that fell that day, both of men and women, were twelve thousand, even all the men of Ai. For Joshua drew not his hand back, wherewith he stretched out the spear, until he had utterly destroyed all the inhabitants of Ai (Joshua 8:1,25-26).

When you rob God, you are under a curse. You will never walk in financial victory until you learn this lesson. God wants you to have a new beginning in your finances, but this blessing only comes through obedience.

SCRIPTURAL GUIDELINES FOR GIVING

Here are nine scriptural guidelines for giving that will launch a new beginning in your finances:

1. Give Willingly

Speak unto the children of Israel, that they bring Me an offering: of every man that giveth it willingly with his heart ye shall take My offering (Exodus 25:2).

For if there be first a willing mind, it is accepted according to that a man hath, and not according to that he hath not (2 Corinthians 8:12).

2. Give Cheerfully

Every man according as he purposeth in his heart, so let him give; not grudgingly, or of necessity: for God loveth a cheerful giver (2 Corinthians 9:7).

3. Give Sacrificially

And He called unto Him His disciples, and saith unto them, Verily I say unto you, That this poor widow hath cast more in, than all they which have cast into the treasury: For all they did cast in of their abundance; but she of her want did cast in all that she had, even all her living (Mark 12:43-44).

4. Give Liberally

The liberal soul shall be made fat: and he that watereth shall be watered also himself (Proverbs 11:25).

He that hath a bountiful eye shall be blessed; for he giveth of his bread to the poor (Proverbs 22:9).

5. Give With Pure Motives

Then the people rejoiced, for that they offered willingly, because with perfect heart they offered willingly to the Lord: and David the king also rejoiced with great joy (1 Chronicles 29:9).

And though I bestow all my goods to feed the poor, and though I give my body to be burned, and have not charity, it profiteth me nothing (1 Corinthians 13:3).

6. Give Your Best

Speak unto Aaron, and to his sons, and unto all the children of Israel, and say unto them, Whatsoever he be of the house of Israel, or of the strangers in Israel, that will offer his oblation for all his vows, and for all his freewill offerings, which they will offer unto the Lord for a burnt offering; Ye shall offer at your own will a male without blemish, of the beeves, of the sheep, or of the goats. But whatsoever hath a blemish, that shall ye not offer: for it shall not be acceptable for you (Leviticus 22:18-20).

7. Give With Simplicity

...he that giveth, let him do it with simplicity (Romans 12:8).

8. Give Without Seeking Recognition

Take heed that ye do not your alms before men, to be seen of them: otherwise ye have no reward of your Father which is in heaven. Therefore when thou doest thine alms, do not sound a trumpet before thee, as the hypocrites do in the synagogues and in the streets, that they may have glory of men. Verily I say unto you, They have their reward. But when thou doest alms, let not thy left hand know what thy right hand doeth:

That thine alms may be in secret: and thy Father which seeth in secret Himself shall reward thee openly (Matthew 6:1-4).

9. Give Expecting God to Meet Your Need

Honour the Lord with thy substance, and with the first-fruits of all thine increase: So shall thy barns be filled with plenty, and thy presses shall burst out with new wine (Proverbs 3:9-10).

But my God shall supply all your need according to His riches in glory by Christ Jesus (Philippians 4:19).

PRACTICAL PRINCIPLES FOR SUPERNATURAL LIVING

In addition to the tremendous scriptural examples and principles we have studied in this chapter, here are some practical guidelines that will assist you in your new beginning financially.

Learn to Live Within Your Means

Live a lifestyle that your income can realistically support. Pride sometimes causes financial difficulties. We buy something because the neighbor got one—a bigger house with a bigger mortgage, a luxury car, a boat, big-screen TV, designer clothes. God wants to bless you and He may provide these luxuries, but He doesn't want your finances dictated by what others are wearing, driving, or living in. Set a realistic budget and learn to live within your means.

Do Not Incur New Debt

It is one thing to embrace the revelation of supernatural debt cancellation as revealed in this chapter, but you must also accept the whole counsel of God. There are other biblical principles that affect our finances. For example, the Bible says: *"Owe no man any thing..."* (Rom. 13:8).

If you live by this principle, then you will not incur credit card debt. While it is convenient to use a credit card for purchases (and you almost have to use one to rent a car or stay in a hotel in America), it can become a snare. The first month that you cannot pay your bill, destroy those credit cards. Trust God for supernatural retirement of your current debt. Make a new beginning by embracing the biblical principle of debt-free living. Do not incur additional debt.

Guard Against Greed and the Love of Money

The Bible declares:

> *But godliness with contentment is great gain. For we brought nothing into this world, and it is certain we can carry nothing out. And having food and raiment let us be therewith content. But they that will be rich fall into temptation and a snare, and into many foolish and hurtful lusts, which drown men in destruction and perdition. For the love of money is the root of all evil: which while some coveted after, they have erred from the faith, and pierced themselves through with many sorrows* (1 Timothy 6:6-10).

Money is not wrong in itself. It is the *love* of money that is the root of all evil and that leads to temptation, snares, and foolish and lustful hurts. The love of money—greed and covetousness—results in debt, causes sorrow, and can even result in erring from the faith.

Jesus warned that riches are deceitful and choke the Word of God out of our lives. (Read Mark 4:18-19.) God wants to bless you, but greediness robs you of contentment:

> *He that loveth silver shall not be satisfied with silver; nor he that loveth abundance with increase: this is also vanity* (Ecclesiastes 5:10).

Reject Condemnation and Embrace Revelation

As you have studied this chapter, you may have identified reasons why you have been struggling financially. Perhaps you have been bound with fear or your focus has been on money instead of the Kingdom. Perhaps you have been living in sin and expecting God's blessings on your finances. You may have robbed God in tithes and offerings and now realize that is why your finances are under a curse. Perhaps you have incurred debt or violated scriptural principles of giving.

The purpose of this chapter is not to bring condemnation, but to point the way to a new beginning in your finances. The Bible declares:

> *There is therefore now no condemnation to them which are in Christ Jesus, who walk not after the flesh, but after the Spirit* (Romans 8:1).

Ask God to forgive you for past scriptural violations, then begin to operate on the basis of the principles you have learned in this chapter. Reject the condemnation of the enemy and embrace this revelation, believing God to plug you into the cycle of supernatural abundance.

You can begin again. Right now. Today. God really does want to give you a new beginning in your finances. He also wants to touch you physically, as well. More about that in Chapter 10.

WALKING IN PHYSICAL HEALTH

You may have been waging a relentless battle in your physical body. Maybe you have endured pain and suffering and been afflicted with chronic sickness, disease, and physical infirmities.

Your resistance has been worn down. You have prayed, fasted, claimed the promises of God, and stood firm on His Word. But you have not yet received the miracle you need. You have almost reached a point where you have lost all hope.

Get ready for a new beginning, a new cycle of healing and restoration in your body.

HOW SICKNESS AND DEATH ENTERED THE WORLD

God never intended His creation to suffer the effects of sin, sickness, or death.

Genesis chapters 1 and 2 record the story of the creation of man. God created man in His own image, breathed into him the breath of life, and man became a living soul. Man was created with a triune nature of body, soul, and spirit.

The body is the physical part of man. The soul and spirit are the spiritual parts that enable him to act, think, feel, react emotionally, and spiritually respond to God. Originally, each part of this triune nature was in harmony with the other two, and the entire triune nature of man was in harmony with God. Man was sinless and healthy in body, soul, and spirit.

Genesis chapter 3, records how Adam and Eve sinned against God by disobeying His Word. Their sin brought the curse of sin, sickness, and death upon all men:

> *Wherefore, as by one man sin entered into the world, and death by sin; and so death passed upon all men, for that all have sinned* (Romans 5:12).

This curse of death was a spiritual separation between man and God as well as physical death that would end a man's life. We can see the effects of the curse immediately in the Genesis record. Adam and Eve hid from God because of the spiritual sickness of sin. Adam blamed Eve, which is the start of emotional sickness resulting from disintegrating relationships. Cain killed Abel, which is an example of social sickness. Physical sickness enters the record through the barrenness of Sarah and the plague upon Abimelech.

When the curse of death came upon man, satan entered the genetic system of the body to begin his destructive mission. The Bible confirms that satan is the source of evil in the world. Jesus said he is a thief and that: *"The thief cometh not, but for to steal, and to kill, and to destroy..."* (John 10:10).

Sickness destroys the body like sin destroys the spirit. Disease steals health, happiness, money, time, effort, and strength. It truly kills and destroys. Because the source of sickness is satan, you must resist it just as you do temptation and sin.

When you resist temptation and sin you are doing spiritual warfare against satan's attacks on your soul and spirit. When you resist sickness you are waging spiritual warfare against his attacks on your physical body.

Every disease comes from a germ of life. Just as your spirit gives life to the body, satan provides the destructive elements of sickness. In the natural world, God takes a living cell and multiplies it to bring forth life and a new child is born. Satan counterfeits this positive process with a negative cycle of his own. He takes a living cell (a virus, cancer, etc.) and multiplies it to bring forth death. This is the spirit of infirmity that works in your body when you are sick. When the spirit of infirmity is cast out, disease in your body dies. As long as that germ exists in the body, the disease lives and continues its destructive work. Although every disease is not a direct attack of demonic spirits, the elements of sickness exist in the world because of satan.

ELIMINATING THE TRADITIONS OF MAN

Jesus told the religious leaders of His time: *"...Thus have ye made the commandment of God of none effect by your tradition"* (Matt. 15:6). If faith comes by hearing God's Word, then it can leave by hearing and accepting traditions of men that destroy faith.

One of the first steps to your new physical beginning is to eliminate these common traditions. Here are the most common ones:

Healing Is Not for Today

Some people claim healing was only for Bible times or for the future when Jesus returns. God says: *"...I am the Lord that healeth thee"* (Exod. 15:26). *I am* is present tense. How can we change it to "I was" (in the past) or "I will be" (in the future)? God has not changed since the beginning of time.

The Bible declares: *"Jesus Christ the same yesterday, and to day, and for ever"* (Heb. 13:8). If the day of miracles is past, then so is the day of salvation, for there is no greater miracle than salvation. If healing is for the future when Jesus returns to earth, then the ministry of teachers, pastors, and other leaders must be for that future time also because the gift of healing is listed in the Bible as a spiritual gift as are these other ministries.

Modern Medicine Makes Divine Healing Unnecessary

Some people believe that there was no competent medical help in the time of Jesus and that now that help is available, we are expected to use it instead of praying to God for healing.

As early as 400 B.C., there was a medical healing science. A man named *Hippocrates* (460-370 B.C.), the father of medicine, developed the science of medicine to a relatively high state. Some of his techniques are still used today. Greece, Egypt, and Rome had many competent practitioners in New Testament times.

Divine healing has nothing to do with the competence or incompetence of medical science. It is a blessing provided in the Atonement. Every good gift comes from God, so it is acceptable to use legitimate medical resources.

Despite the advances of medicine there are still many incurable illnesses so divine healing is still needed. Also, many people are beyond the reach of medical help. For example, in Africa it has been estimated that some 80 percent of the people do not have basic medical care.

The Body Is Emphasized More Than the Soul

Biblical healing deals with the whole man—body, soul, and spirit. Healing is not a gospel of itself; it is only one aspect of the Gospel of Christ. It should never be preached apart from the message of salvation of the souls of sinful men and women.

You Are Sick Because of Your Sin

While all sickness is in the world because of sin, a person is not necessarily sick because of personal sin. Job was a righteous man, yet he suffered physical attacks.

It Is God's Will for You to Be Sick

Have you ever heard this claim? Many do not question whether or not God is able to heal, but whether He is willing. The Bible indicates we are unwise if we do not understand God's will: *"Wherefore be ye not unwise, but understanding what the will of the Lord is"* (Eph. 5:17).

Knowing God's will concerning sickness provides fertile ground on which faith can grow. The prayer of faith is the only prayer that is effective in obtaining healing. You cannot pray with faith when you are wondering if it is God's will to heal.

If you really believe it is God's will for you to be sick, then it is wrong to ask someone to pray for your healing. Those who believe sickness is God's will should not accept medical treatment to get rid of it. They should not let a doctor operate and remove God's will from their body. If you really believe sickness is God's will, you should stop taking medicine and seeing doctors because you would be fighting against the will of God.

But since we know that the source of sickness is satan, then legitimate doctors, medicines, hospitals, and medical science are an extension of the goodness of God. Since sickness is of satan, every legitimate manner of relieving suffering is of God. (By legitimate, we mean those methods that do not involve satanic methods or violate God's Word.)

Healing Is Not for Everyone

If you do not believe that healing is for all, then you must believe that healing is governed by direct revelation in each case as to whether or not it is God's will to heal. You are then relying on direct revelation rather than the written Word of God. You will have no basis for faith until you receive a special revelation in each case that the sick one is among the favored ones to be healed.

This Is an Affliction of the Righteous

Some people say, "Many are the afflictions of the righteous. This is an affliction you must bear because you are righteous."

The meaning of the word *afflictions* that is used in Psalm 34:19 (from where this saying developed) does not refer to physical illness. It refers to trials, hardships, persecutions, or temptations. Even if it did refer to sickness, the remainder of the verse indicates that the Lord wants to deliver you.

In James 5:13-16, a difference is noted between afflictions and sickness. If you are afflicted with trials, persecutions, and temptations, you are to pray for yourself. Although you can ask others to pray with you, they are not called to pray all your troubles away. Scripture instructs you to pray when you are afflicted because you need to learn how to be victorious by praying yourself through trials and temptations. In case of sickness, however, the elders are to be called to pray and the sick are healed.

119

Your Sickness Is Your Cross

The claim that sickness is your cross is easily dealt with. The Cross is not problems, sicknesses, and afflictions that come upon you through no choice of your own. Jesus made it clear that taking up the Cross is a voluntary act, not something you accept because you have no choice. Jesus did not treat sickness and death as a cross sent from God. He treated them as an enemy. If you believe sickness is your cross, then why do you seek medical help to get rid of it?

HOW GOD VIEWS SICKNESS

Once you understand how God views sickness you will never again doubt its source or His desire to heal.

God calls sickness, such as Job experienced, *captivity*: *"And the Lord turned the captivity of Job..."* (Job 42:10).

Jesus came to preach deliverance to the captives:

> *The Spirit of the Lord is upon me, because He hath anointed me to preach the gospel to the poor, He hath sent me to heal the brokenhearted, to preach deliverance to the captives, and recovering of sight to the blind, to set at liberty them that are bruised* (Luke 4:18).

Jesus called sickness *bondage*:

> *And ought not this woman, being a daughter of Abraham, whom Satan hath bound, lo these eighteen years, be loosed from this bond on the sabbath day?* (Luke 13:16)

Jesus viewed sickness as oppression and healed those who were oppressed:

> *How God anointed Jesus of Nazareth with the Holy Ghost and with power; who went about doing good, and healing all that were oppressed of the devil; for God was with Him* (Acts 10:38).

Sickness is called loathsome in the Bible. The Psalmist said: *"For my loins are filled with a loathsome disease; and there is no soundness in my flesh"* (Ps. 38:7). It is also viewed as evil: *"An evil disease, say they, cleaveth fast unto him..."* (Ps. 41:8).

REDEMPTION FROM THE CURSE

Sickness and disease are part of the curse of sin, but Galatians 3:13 declares that: *"Christ has redeemed us from the curse of the law."* When Jesus died on the Cross, He took the curse of sin and death upon Himself.

> *...as by the offense of one* [Adam] *judgment came upon all men to condemnation; even so by the righteousness of One* [Jesus Christ] *the free gift came upon all men unto justification of life. For as by one man's disobedience many were made sinners, so by the obedience of One shall many be made righteous* (Romans 5:18-19).

Salvation and healing are both benefits of the Atonement made on the Cross of Calvary.

Through His death and resurrection, Jesus took the curses of sin, disease, and death in your place. Because He bore the penalty for your sin, you need not bear it. Because He bore your sickness, you need not bear it. Because He rose in resurrection life, you too shall rise! Satan comes to kill, steal, and destroy, but Jesus said: *"...I am come that they might have life, and that they might have it more abundantly"* (John 10:10).

When you receive Jesus as your Savior, the curse of sin is broken. Although you live in a mortal body that is subject to the attacks of both sin and sickness, you are no longer under the curse. Jesus has redeemed you from the curse of the law!

Whenever you question the source of sickness (or anything negative that comes into your life), ask yourself, Does it kill, steal, or destroy? If so, then its source is satan. Does it enable me to live life more abundantly? If so, then its source is God.

Every good gift and every perfect gift is from above, and cometh down from the Father of lights, with whom is no variableness, neither shadow of turning (James 1:17).

Ask yourself: is this physical suffering a good and perfect gift? If you cannot honestly answer yes, then you must accept what the Word says. Sickness is not from God!

HE BORE YOUR SICKNESSES

The reason you can have a new beginning physically is that Jesus bore your sickness:

Surely, He hath borne our griefs, and carried our sorrows; yet we did esteem Him stricken, smitten of God, and afflicted. But He was wounded for our transgressions, He was bruised for our iniquities; the chastisement of our peace was upon Him; and with His stripes we are healed (Isaiah 53:4-5).

Isaiah chapter 53 is a prophetic chapter that refers to Jesus Christ. Verses four and five definitely link healing to the atonement of Jesus by His death on the Cross. The only use of the word *surely* in this chapter, which is a word of emphasis, precedes this provision for our salvation and healing.

Sin and sickness are satan's twin evils. Salvation and healing are God's twin provisions for deliverance. Before Calvary, people were saved and healed by looking forward to the Cross in faith. Afterward, salvation and healing come by looking back to it in faith.

Disease and death entered by sin and are penalties for iniquity, so their remedy must be found in the atonement of Christ. Jesus bore your sicknesses and carried your diseases at the same time and in the same manner that He bore your sins.

That it might be fulfilled which was spoken by Esaias the prophet, saying, Himself took our infirmities and bare our sicknesses (Matthew 8:17).

God laid both sin and sickness on Jesus in the same Atonement. Peter speaks of salvation and healing as being an accomplished fact:

Who His own self bare our sins in His own body on the tree, that we, being dead to sins, should live unto righteousness: by whose stripes ye were healed (1 Peter 2:24).

Since Jesus bore your sins, it must be God's will to save when you come to Him. Since He bore your sicknesses, it must also be His will to heal when you come to Him. The same God who forgives all your sin also heals your diseases:

Bless the Lord, O my soul, and forget not all His benefits: Who forgiveth all thine iniquities, who healeth all thy diseases (Psalm 103:2-3).

The redemptive name *Jehovah-tsidkenu* reveals God's redemptive provision for your soul. The redemptive name *Jehovah-rapha* reveals His redemptive provision for your body.

The word *saved,* used in Romans 10:9, is the same word used by Mark when he said *"...as many as touched him were made whole."* The Greek word *sozo* was used in these passages, and it means "salvation from sin and its penalty." Sickness is part of the penalty, so salvation is part of the atonement for it.

When Jesus died on the Cross, did He take away your sins? Do you, a believer, still battle against sin? The same is true of sickness. Jesus died for your sickness, but as long as you are in an imperfect world, you must also war against sickness.

There is a past, present, and future tense of salvation:

- Past: You have been saved from the penalty of sins committed in the past.

- Present: You are saved from the power of sin in the present.

- Future: You will be saved from the presence of sin in the future (eternity).

The same is true of healing. You are saved from sickness as a penalty for your past sins. You can overcome the power of disease in the present time and be saved from the actual presence of disease in eternity.

ACCEPT THE HEALER AND YOUR HEALING

Since healing is a benefit of the Atonement, you need to accept Jesus not only as your Savior, but also as your Healer. How can He keep you from sin if you have never accepted Him as Savior? How can He keep you from sickness if you have never accepted Him as Healer?

When you pray for healing, pray *"Thy will be done,"* or *"according to Thy will."* Do not say, *"If it be Thy will"* when you are praying for healing and deliverance. A sinner does not pray, "Lord, save me *if* it be Thy will."

Healing is part of the Atonement just like salvation. *If* implies doubt that God wants to make you whole. *According to Thy will* projects confident faith, while leaving the method, extent, and timing to Him.

Jesus taught us to pray, *Thy will be done on earth, as it is in Heaven.* There is no sickness and disease in Heaven, so we can pray confidently against it on earth knowing it is not His will.

Jesus never prayed, "Heal, if it is Your will, God." The only time He prayed, "If it be Thy will" was in relationship to His own submission to the plan of God for His life, not healing. When the phrase, *If you will,* was used by an outcast leper seeking healing, Jesus corrected his uncertainty by assuring him, *I will.* Never turn God's facts into hopes or questions. Act on them as realities, and you will find them to be powerful.

If you are suffering from physical ailments, you can accept Jesus as your Healer, and pray for your healing right now. Place your hand on this page as a point of contact, and pray this prayer aloud:

Father, in the name of Jesus and by the authority of Your Word, I claim my healing right now. Jesus, I confess that by Your stripes I am healed. I accept You as my Healer. I command every sickness, disease, and infirmity to leave my body right now in Jesus' name. I speak health and new life to my body and command it to come into conformity with the Word of God. I praise You that I walk by faith and not by sight. I accept my healing and thank You for it by faith, believing for its full manifestation according to Your Word.

You may not feel any different after you pray this prayer. You may still have physical symptoms, but begin to praise God for your healing. Keep praising Him until what you have believed for in the spiritual world is manifested in the natural world. We walk by faith and not by sight. We base our faith on the Word of God, not on feeling.

It is God's will for you to have a new beginning in your physical body! Be healed, right now, in the name of Jesus Christ!

CHAPTER 11

CONQUERING NEGATIVE CIRCUMSTANCES

We all have them—the difficult, trying, tragic, and annoying situations of life. If you are to have a new beginning, then you must learn how to deal with negative circumstances. You cannot have a new beginning in any of the areas we are talking about unless you learn how to conquer negative circumstances.

Difficult circumstances make you weary and weariness will abort your new beginning and the destiny God has planned for you. The Bible says we are to love God with all our strength:

> *And you shall love the Lord your God with all your heart, with all your soul, with all your mind, and with all your strength. This is the first commandment* (Mark 12:30).

When you are weary and exhausted because of the weight of negative circumstances in your life, your spiritual strength is sapped.

The enemy uses weariness as an opportunity to attack you. Deuteronomy 25:18 (NKJV) records how the enemy met God's people: *...on the way and attacked your rear ranks, all the stragglers at your rear, when you were tired and weary....*

If you are overcome by the daily circumstances of life, you will not be able to move on to greater, new things in God:

If you have run with the footmen, and they have wearied you, then how can you contend with horses? And if in the land of peace, in which you trusted, they wearied you, then how will you do in the floodplain of the Jordan? (Jeremiah 12:5)

One of the chief strategies of the enemy in the endtime is to wear away the saints of God. The Bible says that the spirit of the antichrist: *"...shall speak great words against the most High, and shall wear out the saints of the most High..."* (Dan. 7:25).

YOU ARE NOT ALONE

You are not alone in the battle with your negative circumstances. Your problems are not unique. Many people in the Bible struggled with difficulties.

The psalmist David said: *"I am weary with my groaning; all night I make my bed swim; I drench my couch with my tears"* (Psalm 6:6 NKJV).

Apostle Paul spoke of being in *"...weariness and toil, in sleeplessness often, in hunger and thirst, in fastings often, in cold and nakedness"* (2 Cor. 11:27 NKJV). He said that in Macedonia: *"...our flesh had no rest, but we were troubled on every side; without were fightings, within were fears"* (2 Cor. 7:5). In Asia, Paul said he and his team were *"...burdened beyond measure, above strength, so that we despaired even of life"* (2 Cor. 1:8 NKJV).

Everyone has negative, wearisome circumstances in their lives at times. The Bible explains that: *"Even the youths shall faint and be weary, and the young men shall utterly fall,"* but then boldly declares: *"But those who wait on the Lord shall renew their strength; they shall mount up with wings like eagles, they shall run and not be weary, they shall walk and not faint"* (Isa. 40:30-31 NKJV).

There are many circumstances in life that can prevent you from experiencing a new beginning if you allow them to do so. If you are to experience all God has for you, then you must learn to press beyond these limitations.

BREAKING THROUGH TO VICTORY

In the Book of Mark, there is a story about a lame man who had to break through difficult circumstances in order to receive his new beginning. The circumstances he confronted are similar to those we face, so we can learn from his experience:

> *And again He entered into Capernaum, after some days; and it was noised that He [Jesus] was in the house. And straightway many were gathered together, insomuch that there was no room to receive them, no, not so much as about the door: and He preached the word unto them. And they come unto Him, bringing one sick of the palsy, which was borne of four. And when they could not come nigh unto Him for the press, they uncovered the roof where He was: and when they had broken it up, they let down the bed wherein the sick of the palsy lay. When Jesus saw their faith, He said unto the sick of the palsy, Son, thy sins be forgiven thee. But there were certain of the scribes sitting there, and reasoning in their hearts, Why doth this man thus speak blasphemies? Who can forgive sins but God only? And immediately when Jesus perceived in His spirit that they so reasoned within themselves, He said unto them, Why reason ye these things in your hearts? Whether is it easier to say to the sick of the palsy, Thy sins be forgiven thee; or to say, Arise, and take up thy bed, and walk? But that ye may know that the Son of man hath power on earth to forgive sins, (He saith to the sick of the palsy,) I say unto thee, Arise, and take up thy bed, and go thy way into thine house. And immediately he arose, took up the bed, and went forth before them all; insomuch that they were all amazed, and glorified God, saying, We never saw it on this fashion (Mark 2:1-12).*

A parallel account of this story in Luke 5:17 states that the power of the Lord was present to heal because Jesus was sharing God's Word. When Jesus comes on the scene, He creates expectation that things can change. People are attracted to the Word because of the demonstration of God's power. That's why the house was so crowded.

The Bible says you are the temple of God: *"Know ye not that ye are the temple of God, and that the Spirit of God dwelleth in you?"* (1 Cor. 3:16). The same power of God present in the house that day is present in your spiritual house—and that is all the power you need to overcome negative circumstances.

The sick man in this account had many obstacles to overcome to get to Jesus. The difficult circumstances (the barriers) that he faced are similar to those you must overcome in order to have a new beginning.

BARRIERS TO A NEW BEGINNING

A Human Barrier

There were so many people crowded into this little house that the lame man could not get through to Jesus. They created a human barrier that literally blocked the way to his new beginning.

Think for a minute. What is the human barrier standing between you and your new beginning? Is it words of unbelief spoken by others? People may have spoken negative words over you or said things like, "Things will never change." Perhaps an ungodly relationship with someone is creating circumstances that are blocking your way to a new start.

Don't let anyone tell you things can't change. Don't let anyone stand in the way of your new beginning. Do whatever is necessary to get into the Master's presence and receive your new start.

A Physical Barrier

This man did not have the physical ability to get to the Master. He was bedfast. He was totally hemmed in by his circumstances. This man and his friends would not be stopped, however. The friends took him up to the roof, made an opening, and let him down through it to Jesus.

Whatever it took, this man was determined to have a new beginning. Do you have the same determination?

A Barrier of Tradition

Ripping off the roof and lowering the man to Jesus definitely broke up the order of the service. When you get desperate enough, all you will be concerned about is breaking through the barriers between you and your new beginning.

Religious enemies turned this incident into a theological dispute. You may need to break through the barriers of religion or the rituals with which you were raised in order to eliminate the negative circumstances in your life.

The roof had to be sacrificed. Sometimes you can only break through your negative circumstances by sacrificing your rational, logical, materialistic reasoning. Sometimes it is costly. Ripping up the roof cost someone money!

Are you willing to do whatever it costs to get your new start? Are you willing to lay aside the traditions of religion or culture, the doubts and fears that are keeping you bound to the past and entangled in negative circumstances?

A Barrier of Preconceptions

Sometimes we do not overcome negative circumstances because we try to dictate to God what should be done. We try to tell God what we think needs changing.

The men in this story brought their friend to receive healing. That was the reason they came. They expected Jesus to touch their friend and raise him up. Jesus saw the faith of these men, but there was another barrier—sin.

A Barrier of Sin

The sick man's sin was a major obstacle to his breakthrough to a new life. This man was physically sick, but there was also the spiritual sickness of sin. Jesus dealt with his sin first. He always deals with root causes, not just surface symptoms. In this case, there was a need for an inward change, the forgiveness of his sin. Curing his sin was curing the disease of his soul.

Sin had erected a spiritual barrier between this man and God. We know this by the fact that Jesus forgave his sins in addition to healing his body. Are there spiritual issues of sin, unforgiveness, bitterness, and others that have contributed to your negative circumstances? If so, eliminate these barriers by asking God to forgive you and give you a fresh start.

A Mental Barrier

Perhaps the greatest barrier you will have to break through to change the circumstances of your life is a mental barrier.

The lame man was resigned to being bedfast for the rest of his life. That is the way it had been in the past and that is the way he thought the future would be. That is, until He came to Jesus.

You may have been in your difficult circumstances so long that you have lost hope that things can change. Don't lose hope! It will create a mental barrier to your deliverance.

Hebrews 11:1 says: *"Faith is the substance of things hoped for, the evidence of things not seen."* Hope gives substance to your faith. Without hope, your faith has no substance. If you think things can't change, you are most likely suffering from a hope crisis rather than a faith crisis.

Ask God to eliminate the mental barriers (the spiritual strongholds in your mind) and renew your hope so your faith will have the substance needed to believe for change.

A Barrier of Impossibilities

This man overcame the barrier of impossibilities when he responded in obedience, took up his bed, and walked. Friends can help you to Jesus. They can comfort and stand by you in difficult circumstances. But there comes a time when you must rise up over your circumstances in the power of the Lord.

Jesus told the lame man to arise, take up his bed, and go to his house. Even though he had not walked before, even though mentally it seemed impossible, he immediately responded in obedience. He took up his bed and departed, giving glory to God. Jesus is saying to you today (as He said to this lame man), "Rise up in victory over the circumstances of your life. I want to give you a new start!"

THIS IS THE TIME!

There is another biblical account of a man who broke through the circumstances of his life to embrace a new beginning. His name was *Zacchaeus*, and his story is recorded in Luke:

And Jesus entered and passed through Jericho. And, behold, there was a man named Zacchaeus, which was the chief among the publicans, and he was rich. And he sought to see Jesus who He was; and could not for the press, because he was little of stature. And he ran before, and climbed up into a sycomore tree to see Him: for He was to pass that way. And when Jesus came to the place, He looked up, and saw him, and said unto him, Zacchaeus, make haste, and come down; for to day I must abide at thy house. And he made haste, and came down, and received Him joyfully. And when they saw it, they all murmured, saying, That He was gone to be guest with a man that is a sinner. And Zacchaeus stood, and said unto the Lord; Behold, Lord, the half of my goods I give to the poor; and if I have taken any thing from any man by false accusation, I restore him fourfold. And Jesus said unto him, This day is salvation come to this house, forsomuch as he also is a son of Abraham. For the Son of man is come to seek and to save that which was lost (Luke 19:1-10).

Zacchaeus was a tax collector. He may not have been an honest man, a religious man, or a loved man, but he was a man who recognized the move of God. It was the hour of opportunity for a change in his life because Jesus was passing through town.

There are times and seasons in the move of God and you don't want to miss these. Ecclesiastes 3:1 declares: *"To every thing there is a season, and a time to every purpose under the heaven."* Galatians 4:4-5 explains that it was in the *fullness of time* that God sent His Son to redeem us.

Receive this word of admonition today: Jesus is entering into the midst of your circumstances. What happens while He is there depends on you.

TWO MAJOR OBSTACLES

Zacchaeus had a burning desire to see Jesus. He wanted a change in his life, but there were two major obstacles he had to overcome: the crowd around him and his stature.

The Crowd Around Him

As in the account of the lame man, the press of the crowd was a barrier Zacchaeus had to overcome to get to the Master. The same is true for you. You must bypass negative people around you, those who say that circumstances cannot change, in order to begin again. You must listen for the voice of the Master above the roar of the crowd. He says you can have a new beginning.

His Stature

Zacchaeus was too short: *"And he sought to see Jesus who he was; and could not for the press, because he was little of stature"* (Luke 19:3). Zacchaeus did not let his lack of height keep him from the Master. He ran, found a tree, and climbed up into it.

The Bible says we are all too short to change our circumstances because *"...all have sinned, and come short of the glory of God"* (Rom. 3:23). Whatever shortness is in your life that is keeping you mired in your negative circumstances, determine that right now—today—you will press through the obstacles to get to the Master. Like Zacchaeus, you must take the initiative if you want things to change.

Zacchaeus needed a tree in order to meet his Savior. God planted that sycamore tree a long time before Zacchaeus needed it. I think God planted it there with Zacchaeus in mind.

God planted a tree for you, too. It is the tree of Calvary. It is the spiritual tree to which you must come for your new beginning. God has planted the tree, but you must come to it and embrace it in order to have a new beginning.

In order to reach the tree of his destiny, Zacchaeus shed his dignity. Zacchaeus was a tax collector. He was a chief among the publicans. He was rich. He laid aside his wealth, position, and education. He abandoned it all and climbed a tree. How undignified!

Let me ask you. How desperate are you for your circumstances to change? Will you do whatever God asks of you even if it seems strange? Zacchaeus acted on his desperation. He knew he must see this Man who could change everything. Zacchaeus ran. Zacchaeus climbed. Zacchaeus did whatever was necessary to get to the Master.

And when Jesus came to the place, he looked up, and saw him, and said unto him, Zacchaeus, make haste, and come down; for to day I must abide at thy house (Luke 19:5).

HE KNOWS WHERE YOU ARE

Whether you are a believer suffering innocently in negative circumstances or a sinner suffering the effects of your sin, Jesus knows exactly where you are. God knew where Adam and Eve were, even when He cried out, "Where are you?" He simply wants you to acknowledge where you are. It doesn't matter if you are depressed, discouraged, in bondage, or in sin. You can't receive His help if you don't acknowledge your need.

When Jesus encountered Zacchaeus, He didn't set an appointment to see him two weeks later. He made him a priority. God is available for your need today. He is ready to change your circumstances and give you a new beginning.

Jesus told Zacchaeus to make haste and come down from the tree. Don't lag behind when God passes your way as He is doing right now through the pages of this chapter. Don't rationalize it. Don't analyze what God is saying. Don't stay where you are, lamenting over your shortcomings.

Jesus told Zacchaeus, "Today is the day. I'm coming to your house. Things are about to change right now!"

Do you want a change in your circumstances now or later? Today or someday? The key to spiritual victories is timing. Now is the time for your deliverance. This is your day for things to change! Don't miss the move of God.

Zacchaeus abandoned his old way of life, his old routines of living, thinking, and functioning. That is what it is going to take to effect true change. You must abandon every sinful lifestyle, every negative thought, every carnal way of operating, and break through every negative circumstance. Zacchaeus declared: "*...Behold, Lord, the half of my goods I give to the poor; and if I have taken any thing from any man by false accusation, I restore him fourfold*" (Luke 19:8). His new beginning was evidenced by a changed life. Yours will be, too!

SEVEN STEPS TO CHANGE

Let's examine one other biblical account that provides practical steps for changing your circumstances. These steps are drawn from the story of blind Bartimaeus:

> *And they came to Jericho: and as he went out of Jericho with his disciples and a great number of people, blind Bartimaeus, the son of Timaeus, sat by the highway side begging. And when he heard that it was Jesus of Nazareth, he began to cry out, and say, Jesus, thou Son of David, have mercy on me. And many charged him that he should hold his peace: but he cried the more a great deal, Thou Son of David, have mercy on me. And Jesus stood still, and commanded him to be called. And they call the blind man, saying unto him, Be of good comfort, rise; He calleth thee. And he, casting away his garment, rose, and came to Jesus. And Jesus answered and said unto him, What wilt thou that I should do unto thee? The blind man said unto him, Lord, that I might receive my sight. And Jesus said unto him, Go thy way; thy faith hath made thee whole. And immediately he received his sight, and followed Jesus in the way* (Mark 10:46-52).

Step 1: Assume Responsibility for the Circumstances in Your Life

By assuming responsibility, it does not necessarily mean that the circumstances in which you are entangled are your fault. The word *responsibility* simply means the "ability to respond."

Bartimaeus was not responsible for his physical condition, but took the responsibility that things could change. He realized, I am blind, I am a beggar, and I want things to change! If you want to position yourself for new things, then you must admit that your present circumstances need to change.

Step 2: Believe That Things Can Change

Bartimaeus had been sitting there for years, blind and a beggar. You may have been in your negative circumstance for years. Your health problem may be chronic. You may have been in therapy for mental or emotional conditions for a decade. You may have lived in poverty all of your life and been trapped in a bad relationship for years. Change will only come when you have the faith to believe that things *can* change. If you don't have faith, then pray as the man in Mark 9:24: *"...Lord I believe; help thou mine unbelief."*

Step 3: Cry out to God

Bartimaeus began to cry out because he believed things could change. If you don't cry out for change, then things will remain as they are. Where has your silence gotten you? Where has your refusal to deal with the circumstances in your life gotten you?

When you cry out to Jesus, He will change your circumstances. You may think, like Bartimaeus, that you are lost in the crowd, but He knows right where you are. Keep on crying out to Him until things change. But remember: Crying alone isn't enough. You must cry to someone who can do something about your need. That Someone is Jesus!

Step 4: Clarify What You Need

In the past, Bartimaeus asked for money, but this time he didn't ask for alms. He wanted a new life.

Have you been asking for the wrong thing? Perhaps you have been seeking rehabilitation, but what you need is change—not rehabilitation of the old, not a better way of life, not more counseling. You need a brand new life:

> *Therefore if any man be in Christ, he is a new creature: old things are passed away; behold, all things are become new* (2 Corinthians 5:17).

Bartimaeus clarified what he needed when Jesus asked him, "What do you want?" Bartimaeus replied, "I'm blind. I want to see!" Express to God exactly what you need. What are the circumstances in your life that need to change?

Step 5: Don't Let Others Discourage You

Many in the crowd told Bartimaeus to be quiet, but he didn't care what the many said because the majority is not always right. It doesn't matter what the majority says about your circumstances. It only matters what God says.

Sometimes, even your dearest friends will stand in the way of your miracle. They may say, "Things can't change. It can't be done. It's never been done." If, like Bartimaeus, you were born that way, or if you have lived in terrible circumstances for years, things *can* change. You *can* have a new beginning!

Bartimaeus got to the place that he said, "I don't care what anyone thinks. I'm tired of going through life a blind beggar!" That is the same point to which you must come.

Step 6: Persevere Through the Circumstances

It was crowded, noisy, hard to be heard, and people were telling him to shut up, but Bartimaeus didn't care. The circumstances weren't ideal for his deliverance. If you are waiting for ideal circumstances to change your life, it is not going to happen. It is in the midst of difficult circumstances that miracles are manifested.

Step 7: Leave the Old Behind to Embrace the New

Bartimaeus wore a garment that identified him as a blind beggar, similar to how carrying a white cane or walking with a guide dog marks a blind person in society today. When Jesus called to him, Bartimaeus did something bold. He cast this garment aside. He cut his ties to the past. He threw off the symbol of his bondage. He made no provisions for failure.

If you are to leave your negative circumstances behind, you will have to do something bold. You must take a step of faith and make no provisions for failure. You must have no plans to go back to the old way of life, the old situations, the old bondages.

Jesus told Bartimaeus that his faith had made him whole. That faith was demonstrated as Bartimaeus stepped out and left behind the garments that chained him to his past. The change in his life was immediate. The Scriptures say that he received his sight immediately.

WHICH BARRIERS ARE BLOCKING YOUR WAY?

Which of the barriers discussed in this chapter are blocking your way to victory over your circumstances? What is standing between you and your miracle, your healing, the restoration of your relationships, your hopes and dreams, your ministry? What are the negative circumstances that have you trapped and bound?

This is the time for your deliverance! Your physical, mental, or emotional condition is not too big for God. Your poverty is not too deep. Your habit is not too great. Determine right now that you will break through every barrier. Begin to raise the roof spiritually, so to speak, to break through to victory. Ask God to help you identify and deal with every barrier satan has erected through the negative circumstances of your life. God's Word to you today is:

> *ARISE [from the depression and prostration in which circumstances have kept you—rise to a new life]! Shine (be radiant with the glory of the Lord), for your light has come, and the glory of the Lord has risen upon you!* ([Zech. 8:23] Isaiah 60:1 AMP).

Accept this prophetic admonition from the Lord:

> *Don't look to the bigness of your need, look to the bigness of your God. Your circumstances are hindrances to seeing my abilities. If you keep your eyes on your circumstances, the devil will use your circumstances to defeat you and accuse the Word of God, the written and living Word. Your victory is keeping your eyes on the bigness of your God and His ability. He has promised to take you step by step by step, not all at once, but step by step, and each step will be a miracle!*

This is the Word of God to you today. Don't look to your circumstances or your need. Look to your God! He will lead you, step by step, to a new beginning. Even if your circumstances have resulted in tremendous losses, you can experience total restoration. Chapter 12 describes the process.

RESTORING ALL THAT THE ENEMY HAS STOLEN

Do you feel as if you have lost everything, and there is no hope?

- You may be sitting in a lonely prison cell.

- You may have lost your home, your business, and your finances.

- Your family may have abandoned you.

- You may be suffering emotionally, mentally, and physically.

God wants to restore everything the enemy has stolen from you! In this chapter, we will look at two men—Job and David—who lost everything yet persevered to receive total restoration. We will also identify eight keys to restoration drawn from their stories that will enable you to claim total restoration in your own life.

JOB LOST IT ALL

Job is a classic example of a man who lost everything. The Bible says that Job was a righteous man, one who feared and served God:

There was a man in the land of Uz, whose name was Job; and that man was perfect and upright, and one that feared God, and eschewed evil (Job 1:1).

Job had many possessions and a great family. Most of all, he feared and served God:

And there were born unto him seven sons and three daughters. His substance also was seven thousand sheep, and three thousand camels, and five hundred yoke of oxen, and five hundred she asses, and a very great household; so that this man was the greatest of all the men of the east. And his sons went and feasted in their houses, every one his day; and sent and called for their three sisters to eat and to drink with them. And it was so, when the days of their feasting were gone about, that Job sent and sanctified them, and rose up early in the morning, and offered burnt offerings according to the number of them all: for Job said, It may be that my sons have sinned, and cursed God in their hearts. Thus did Job continually (Job 1:2-5).

There came a day when everything changed:

Now there was a day when the sons of God came to present themselves before the Lord, and Satan came also among them. And the Lord said unto Satan, Whence comest thou? Then Satan answered the Lord, and said, From going to and fro in the earth, and from walking up and down in it. And the Lord said unto Satan, Hast thou considered my servant Job, that there is none like him in the earth, a perfect and an upright man, one that feareth God, and escheweth evil? Then Satan answered the Lord, and said, Doth Job fear God for nought? Hast not Thou made an hedge about him, and about his house, and about all that he hath on every side? Thou hast blessed the work of his hands, and his substance is increased in the land. But put forth Thine hand now, and touch all that he hath, and he will curse Thee to Thy face. And the Lord said unto Satan, Behold, all that he hath is in thy power; only upon himself put not forth thine hand. So Satan went forth from the presence of the Lord (Job 1:6-12).

Satan's contention was that Job was so blessed that, of course, he would naturally love and serve God. With God's permission, satan was allowed to attack Job through the circumstances of his life.

First, in a series of devastating blows, Job lost his earthly possessions:

And there came a messenger unto Job, and said, The oxen were plowing, and the asses feeding beside them: And the Sabeans fell upon them, and took them away; yea, they have slain the servants with the edge of the sword; and I only am escaped alone to tell thee. While he was yet speaking, there came also another, and said, The fire of God is fallen from heaven, and hath burned up the sheep, and the servants, and consumed them; and I only am escaped alone to tell thee. While he was yet speaking, there came also another, and said, The Chaldeans made out three bands, and fell upon the camels, and have carried them away, yea, and slain the servants with the edge of the sword; and I only am escaped alone to tell thee (Job 1:14-17).

Next, Job lost his children:

While he was yet speaking, there came also another, and said, Thy sons and thy daughters were eating and drinking wine in their eldest brother's house: And, behold, there came a great wind from the wilderness, and smote the four corners of the house, and it fell upon the young men, and they are dead; and I only am escaped alone to tell thee (Job 1:18-19).

Then satan appeared again before God and challenged:

> *Again there was a day when the sons of God came to present themselves before the Lord, and Satan came also among them to present himself before the Lord. And the Lord said unto Satan, From whence comest thou? And Satan answered the Lord, and said, From going to and fro in the earth, and from walking up and down in it. And the Lord said unto Satan, Hast thou considered my servant Job, that there is none like him in the earth, a perfect and an upright man, one that feareth God, and escheweth evil? and still he holdeth fast his integrity, although thou movedst Me against him, to destroy him without cause. And Satan answered the Lord, and said, Skin for skin, yea, all that a man hath will he give for his life. But put forth Thine hand now, and touch his bone and his flesh, and he will curse Thee to thy face. And the Lord said unto Satan, Behold, he is in Thine hand; but save his life* (Job 2:1-6).

Then Job lost his health:

> *...Satan...went from the presence of the Lord, and smote Job with sore boils from the sole of his foot unto his crown* (Job 2:7).

Finally, Job lost the comfort and support of his wife, who said:

> *Dost thou still retain thine integrity? curse God, and die* (Job 2:9).

Job also had to contend with the negative attitudes of his friends who accused him of sin and were judgmental and uncompassionate. You can read their extensive dialogues in Job 2-37.

Job's losses were staggering and they occurred in such quick succession that before he could recover from one blow, another was delivered. Job lost everything except his faith in God. His first response to these tragedies was to worship God and declare His righteous judgments:

> ...*arose, and rent his mantle, and shaved his head, and fell down upon the ground, and worshipped, And said, Naked came I out of my mother's womb, and naked shall I return thither: the Lord gave, and the Lord hath taken away; blessed be the name of the Lord. In all this Job sinned not, nor charged God foolishly* (Job 1:20-22).

Later, at one point in his intense suffering, Job could no longer even sense God's presence:

> *Behold, I go forward, but He is not there; and backward, but I cannot perceive Him: On the left hand, where He doth work, but I cannot behold him: He hideth Himself on the right hand, that I cannot see Him* (Job 23:8-9).

Yet, in the midst of this, Job declared:

> *But He knoweth the way that I take: when He hath tried me, I shall come forth as gold. My foot hath held His steps, His way have I kept, and not declined. Neither have I gone back from the commandment of His lips; I have esteemed the words of His mouth more than my necessary food* (Job 23:10-12).

Stripped of his possessions, suffering agonizing pain, forsaken by his family and friends, Job eventually became weary and lost hope. He even cursed the day he was born:

> *Let the day perish wherein I was born, and the night in which it was said, There is a man child conceived. Let that day be darkness; let not God regard it from above, neither let the light shine upon it. Let darkness and the shadow of death stain it; let a cloud*

dwell upon it; let the blackness of the day terrify it. As for that night, let darkness seize upon it; let it not be joined unto the days of the year, let it not come into the number of the months. Lo, let that night be solitary, let no joyful voice come therein. Let them curse it that curse the day, who are ready to raise up their mourning. Let the stars of the twilight thereof be dark; let it look for light, but have none; neither let it see the dawning of the day: Because it shut not up the doors of my mother's womb, nor hid sorrow from mine eyes. Why died I not from the womb? why did I not give up the ghost when I came out of the belly? (Job 3:3-11)

Job lost everything. When he turned his eyes on his losses, he became despondent and lost hope. Job didn't have the Book of Job like we do. He couldn't see behind the scenes as we are privileged to do through the pages of God's Word. He didn't realize that there was a spiritual reason behind the circumstances he was experiencing in the natural world. We are privileged to that knowledge through Job chapters 1 and 2, where the spiritual battle that was raging over Job is recorded.

As you face your losses, you must understand that there is a spiritual battle raging over you also. Satan wants your worship, your allegiance, and your very life. Worship is what he craved from the time he ascended in the heavenlies and tried to take God's place. Lucifer said in his heart:

...I will ascend into heaven, I will exalt my throne above the stars of God: I will sit also upon the mount of the congregation, in the sides of the north: I will ascend above the heights of the clouds; I will be like the most High (Isaiah 14:13-14).

Always remember that behind every negative circumstance in your life, satan is warring for your mind, your body, and your very soul. In the end, Job recovered all he had lost in this time of intense suffering. In fact:

...the Lord gave Job twice as much as he had before. Then came there unto him all his brethren, and all his sisters, and

all they that had been of his acquaintance before, and did eat bread with him in his house: and they bemoaned him, and comforted him over all the evil that the Lord had brought upon him: every man also gave him a piece of money, and every one an earring of gold. So the Lord blessed the latter end of Job more than his beginning: for he had fourteen thousand sheep, and six thousand camels, and a thousand yoke of oxen, and a thousand she asses. He had also seven sons and three daughters. And he called the name of the first, Jemima; and the name of the second, Kezia; and the name of the third, Keren-happuch. And in all the land were no women found so fair as the daughters of Job: and their father gave them inheritance among their brethren. After this lived Job an hundred and forty years, and saw his sons, and his sons' sons, even four generations. So Job died, being old and full of days (Job 42:10-17).

DAVID LOST IT ALL

David is another man who lost it all and experienced total restoration. When David was forced to flee for his life from King Saul, he took refuge in a town called Ziklag. This was a town controlled by Israel's enemy, and it wasn't really a good move for David to make:

And it was told Saul that David was fled to Gath: and he sought no more again for him. And David said unto Achish, If I have now found grace in thine eyes, let them give me a place in some town in the country, that I may dwell there: for why should thy servant dwell in the royal city with thee? Then Achish gave him Ziklag that day: wherefore Ziklag pertaineth unto the kings of Judah unto this day. And the time that David dwelt in the country of the Philistines was a full year and four months (1 Samuel 27:4-7).

In an attempt to prove his allegiance, David began to battle Achish's enemies. In First Samuel chapter 27, it is recorded how David and his men invaded the Beshurites, the Gezerites, and the Amalekites. After a series of victorious battles, David and his men returned to their city of Ziklag to find total devastation:

> And it came to pass, when David and his men were come to Ziklag on the third day, that the Amalekites had invaded the south, and Ziklag, and smitten Ziklag, and burned it with fire; And had taken the women captives, that were therein: they slew not any, either great or small, but carried them away, and went on their way. So David and his men came to the city, and, behold, it was burned with fire; and their wives, and their sons, and their daughters, were taken captives. Then David and the people that were with him lifted up their voice and wept, until they had no more power to weep. And David's two wives were taken captives, Ahinoam the Jezreelitess, and Abigail the wife of Nabal the Carmelite (1 Samuel 30:1-5).

David's safe haven of Ziklag was in total ruins and the families of his men had been taken captive, including David's two wives.

> And David was greatly distressed; for the people spake of stoning him, because the soul of all the people was grieved, every man for his sons and for his daughters: but David encouraged himself in the Lord his God. And David said to Abiathar the priest, Ahimelech's son, I pray thee, bring me hither the ephod. And Abiathar brought thither the ephod to David. And David inquired at the Lord, saying, Shall I pursue after this troop? shall I overtake them? And he answered him, Pursue: for thou shalt surely overtake them, and without fail recover all (1 Samuel 30:6-8).

David's men were so upset about their losses that they spoke of stoning him, but in the midst of total devastation, David encouraged himself in God.

Then he sent for the priest and the ephod to seek God's guidance. God told him to pursue the enemy, overtake them, and recover all, which he did:

> *And David recovered all that the Amalekites had carried away: and David rescued his two wives. And there was nothing lacking to them, neither small nor great, neither sons nor daughters, neither spoil, nor any thing that they had taken to them: David recovered all* (1 Samuel 30:18-19).

STEPS TO TOTAL RESTORATION

Job was a righteous man who lost everything and persevered to recover all the enemy destroyed. David, who most likely was out of God's perfect will living in the land of Israel's enemy, recovered all after his devastating loss. What can we learn from these examples that will enable us to experience total restoration?

There are eight spiritual keys revealed in the stories of Job and David that led to their restoration. These steps—applied spiritually—will enable you to experience total restoration also, whether you have lost all innocently or whether your own decisions have resulted in your losses.

Step 1: Repent and Ask God's Forgiveness

If your losses are due to your own sins or bad decisions, repent, and ask God's forgiveness.

You may also need to repent, as Job did, for wrong attitudes. After God answered Job's many complaints in a lengthy dialogue (see Job 38-42), Job declared: *"Wherefore I abhor myself, and repent in dust and ashes..."* (Job 42:6).

When you are in a difficult situation it is easy to fall into fear, doubt, and unbelief and say things you shouldn't. Ask God to forgive you.

Step 2: Forgive Others

You may need to forgive others who have contributed to your suffering. God directed Job to intercede for his friends—Eliphaz, the Temanite, and Bildad, the Shuhite—who were accusing, judgmental, and extremely uncompassionate during his ordeal:

> *And it was so, that after the Lord had spoken these words unto Job, the Lord said to Eliphaz the Temanite, My wrath is kindled against thee, and against thy two friends: for ye have not spoken of me the thing that is right, as my servant Job hath. Therefore take unto you now seven bullocks and seven rams, and go to my servant Job, and offer up for yourselves a burnt offering; and my servant Job shall pray for you: for him will I accept: lest I deal with you after your folly, in that ye have not spoken of me the thing which is right, like my servant Job. So Eliphaz the Temanite and Bildad the Shuhite and Zophar the Naamathite went, and did according as the Lord commanded them: the Lord also accepted Job. And the Lord turned the captivity of Job, when he prayed for his friends: also the Lord gave Job twice as much as he had before* (Job 42:7-10).

Job's restoration was linked to forgiveness and your restoration may be also. What good things might God be waiting to restore to you that are being hindered by your unforgiveness? By an act of your will, forgive. Your own forgiveness is vitally linked to your willingness to forgive others:

> *For if ye forgive men their trespasses, your heavenly Father will also forgive you: But if ye forgive not men their trespasses, neither will your Father forgive your trespasses* (Matthew 6:14-15).

Unforgiveness blocks the total restoration God wants you to experience.

Step 3: *Worship Your Way Through It*

We find Job worshiping God in chapter 1 when he lost all, and worshiping again in chapter 42 when everything was restored. Even when he could not feel God's presence, Job declared:

But he knoweth the way that I take: when he hath tried me, I shall come forth as gold. My foot hath held his steps, his way have I kept, and not declined. Neither have I gone back from the commandment of his lips; I have esteemed the words of his mouth more than my necessary food (Job 23:10-12).

When confronted with devastating loss, David also *"…encouraged himself in the Lord his God"* (1 Sam. 30:6).

You may wonder, *How I can I praise God when I have lost everything?* You can praise Him because He is still in control. We learn from Job's story that God limits the circumstances satan brings into your life. God is in control of your circumstances, even if you have lost everything. There is no loss that comes into your life of which God is not aware. Satan cannot touch you without permission from God. (Read Job 1:8-12.)

You are assured, also, that God will never allow circumstances that you are unable to bear:

For no temptation (no trial regarded as enticing to sin), [no matter how it comes or where it leads] has overtaken you and laid hold on you that is not common to man [that is, no temptation or trial has come to you that is beyond human resistance and that is not adjusted and adapted and belonging to human experience, and such as man can bear]. But God is faithful [to His Word and to His compassionate nature], and He [can be trusted] not to let you be tempted and tried and assayed beyond your ability and strength of resistance and power to endure, but with the temptation He will [always] also provide the way out (the means of escape to a landing place), that you may be capable and strong and powerful to bear up under it patiently (1 Corinthians 10:13 AMP).

You can worship your way through your difficulties because you know God has a plan to use every loss you experience:

But as for you, ye thought evil against me; but God meant it unto good, to bring to pass, as it is this day, to save much people alive (Genesis 50:20).

Every circumstance that enters your life will be turned for good:

And we know that all things work together for good to them that love God, to them who are the called according to His purpose (Romans 8:28).

Settle it in your heart. It is satan who comes to kill, steal, and destroy—not God. Jesus wants you to have abundant life:

The thief cometh not, but for to steal, and to kill, and to destroy: I am come that they might have life, and that they might have it more abundantly (John 10:10).

God's ultimate purpose for you is good:

Every good gift and every perfect gift is from above, and cometh down from the Father of lights, with whom is no variableness, neither shadow of turning (James 1:17).

James said to count it joy when you encounter difficulties:

Consider it wholly joyful, my brethren, whenever you are enveloped in or encounter trials of any sort or fall into various temptations. Be assured and understand that the trial and proving of your faith bring out endurance and steadfastness and patience. But let endurance and steadfastness and patience have full play and do a thorough work, so that you may be [people] perfectly and fully developed [with no defects], lacking in nothing (James 1:2-4 AMP).

You can rejoice in God and worship Him not *for* your losses, but for the promised outcome. Your faith will be proven. All will be turned for your good. You will learn endurance, steadfastness, and patience. In the end, you will lack nothing!

Step 4: *Focus on God*

Turn your eyes from your circumstances and fix them upon God and His Word. Set your mind on God's faithfulness and allow His peace to guard your heart and mind:

> *Thou wilt keep him in perfect peace, whose mind is stayed on thee: because he trusteth in thee. Trust ye in the Lord for ever: for in the Lord Jehovah is everlasting strength* (Isaiah 26:3-4).

Despite Job's suffering, he continued to focus on God. When Job lost everything, he *"...arose, and rent his mantle, and shaved his head, and fell down upon the ground, and worshipped"* (Job 1:20). He declared concerning God's Word: *"Neither have I gone back from the commandment of his lips; I have esteemed the words of his mouth more than my necessary food"* (Job 23:12). Get into the Word of God. Esteem it more than your necessary food!

In the midst of his losses and facing possible death, David's focus was on God as he encouraged himself in the Lord. He also sought new direction from God as he called for the priest and the ephod, which in those days were used to seek God's will.

Seek God's direction, knowing that He will show you the way to a new beginning and total restoration:

> *And thine ears shall hear a word behind thee, saying, This is the way, walk ye in it, when ye turn to the right hand, and when ye turn to the left* (Isaiah 30:21).

Step 5: *Resist the Enemy*

David rose up and pursued the enemy, taking back all that had been stolen. Don't remain in the ashes of your losses: *"Submit yourselves therefore to God. Resist the devil, and he will flee from you"* (James 4:7).

Cast out fear, worry, and doubt in the name of Jesus. Bind the work of the enemy in your circumstances. Use the spiritual armor described in Ephesians chapter 6 to war against the attacks of the enemy.

Step 6: Release Your Faith

Release your faith for total restoration of all the enemy has stolen from you. Act upon what you believe God for as if it were already done. Be like faithful Abraham who:

> ...believed, even God, who quickeneth the dead, and calleth those things which be not as though they were. Who against hope believed in hope, that he might become the father of many nations; according to that which was spoken, So shall thy seed be. And being not weak in faith, he considered not his own body now dead, when he was about an hundred years old, neither yet the deadness of Sara's womb: He staggered not at the promise of God through unbelief; but was strong in faith, giving glory to God; And being fully persuaded that, what He had promised, He was able also to perform (Romans 4:17-21).

Believe God for total restoration in your life:

> And I will restore to you the years that the locust hath eaten, the cankerworm, and the caterpillar, and the palmerworm... (Joel 2:25).

Step 7: Wait on the Lord

Job waited a long time, but finally God intervened in his circumstances. Do not become weary of waiting, but: "...consider him that endured such contradiction of sinners against himself, lest ye be wearied and faint in your minds" (Heb. 12:3).

Wait on God in prayer, worship, and Bible study, knowing that:

He giveth power to the faint; and to them that have no might He increaseth strength. Even the youths shall faint and be weary, and the young men shall utterly fall: But they that wait upon the Lord shall renew their strength; they shall mount up with wings as eagles; they shall run, and not be weary; and they shall walk, and not faint (Isaiah 40:29-31).

Step 8: Persevere

Regardless of how long you must wait for God to move in your circumstances, regardless of the greatness of your losses and the pain and heartache you have suffered, continue to persevere for total restoration. Keep believing and releasing your faith, expecting God to restore all. Both Job and David experienced total restoration. So can you!

Here is God's Word to you:

Instead of your [former] shame you shall have a twofold recompense; instead of dishonor and reproach [your people] shall rejoice in their portion. Therefore in their land they shall possess double [what they had forfeited]; everlasting joy shall be theirs (Isaiah 61:7 AMP).

God wants to restore double what you forfeited, even if (as you will learn in the next chapter) your losses were due to your own actions. You can experience total restoration, a brand-new beginning!

CHAPTER 13

ACCEPTING GOD'S SECOND CHANCE

The Bible is filled with examples of those who accepted a second chance from God for a new beginning. As we are learning, these men and women discovered that despite their past failures, they could begin again.

God is the God of a second chance. No matter how many times you try and seemingly fail, never give up. You only fail when you quit trying. Like each of the examples we have studied so far, you can begin again.

In this chapter, however, we will discuss a different type of person who needs a new beginning. It is the person who has deliberately walked away from God. This is not a Moses or a John Mark, who tried and failed. It is the person who purposefully turns their back on God. Can such a person really have a new beginning when the person has experienced the wonderful things of God and then deliberately walked away from the Father's house?

THE PARABLE OF THE PRODIGAL SON

Luke chapter 15 records the account of what has come to be known as the story of the prodigal son. In the first two verses, Luke gives the setting for the story:

> *Then drew near unto him all the publicans and sinners for to hear him. And the Pharisees and scribes murmured, saying,*

This man receiveth sinners, and eateth with them (Luke 15:1-2).

Jesus uses three parables to address the self-righteous, legalistic attitudes of the Pharisees. A *parable* is an "analogy." It is where you place something alongside of something else to make an association or comparison between them. A simple definition is that they are earthly stories with heavenly meanings.

The three parables that follow this introduction are the Lord's response to the murmurings of the Pharisees regarding sinners. Jesus tells the story of a lost sheep (see Luke 15:3-7); a lost coin (see Luke 15:8-10); and a lost son (see Luke 15:11-16). In each example, the love and compassion of God for lost and hurting humanity is emphasized.

The first two parables emphasize God's love and concern for lost souls. The third emphasizes the fact that not only will God save a sinner, He will take back a son or daughter who has strayed. He will give them a second chance.

If you have walked away from the Father's house, if you are backslidden and disillusioned, living far from the Father, then this message for you. You can return to the Father's house.

LEAVING THE FATHER'S HOUSE

And he said, A certain man had two sons: And the younger of them said to his father, Father, give me the portion of goods that falleth to me. And he divided unto them his living. And not many days after the younger son gathered all together, and took his journey into a far country, and there wasted his substance with riotous living. And when he had spent all, there arose a mighty famine in that land; and he began to be in want. And he went and joined himself to a citizen of that country; and he sent him into his fields to feed swine. And he would fain have filled his belly with the husks that the swine did eat: and no man gave unto him (Luke 15:11-16).

Unlike the two previous parables in this chapter concerning the lost sheep and the lost coin, this parable relates the story of a young man who lived in his Father's house. He was not lost. He was a son. He had a divine destiny and was an heir of his father. He enjoyed the good life in his father's kingdom.

One day, this young man told his father: "Give me my inheritance now. Give me my freedom." Why did he want to leave his father's house, with all of its rich provisions? We are not specifically told. Perhaps he didn't like the rules or didn't trust his father's management. Maybe he thought he was missing out on the good things in life. Perhaps he was tired of living in the shadow of his older brother. Maybe he wanted to manage his own life and do his own thing.

These are the same reasons why men and women leave the heavenly Father's house spiritually. Some turn against God when something happens in their lives that they don't understand. They don't trust God's management of their life. Others don't like the rules. Some feel that they don't measure up to other believers in the house. Some, who believe they are missing out on the good things in life, decide they want to manage their own lives and do their own thing.

Despite the son's rebellion, the father was good to him. He gave him his inheritance, which was contrary to the customs of the time. Despite our rebellion, God is good to us. It is His goodness, not wrath, that draws people to repentance:

> ...*do you despise the riches of His goodness, forbearance, and longsuffering, not knowing that the goodness of God leads you to repentance?* (Romans 2:4 NKJV)

LIFE IN THE FAR COUNTRY

This young man went to a far country. When you walk away from God, that is exactly where you are spiritually. There, he lived riotously with loose, reckless, extravagant living. He had lots of friends, and the good times rolled—for a season, but riotous living always comes to an end. It always leaves a man hungry and unfulfilled.

The young man wasted his entire inheritance. If you are not in the Father's house, then you are wasting your substance. Your sinful state is a waste of energy, health, talents, and your destiny. What you perceive as the good times will ultimately come to a bitter end.

Eventually, a famine came to the country where the young man lived. Your famine may be a disaster, an accident, or sickness. God did not cause it, but He will use it to drive you back to your heavenly Father's house.

This young man lost everything—his home, his money, his friends, and his provisions. He lost everything, except one thing. He did not lose His father's love. Perhaps that describes you. You may have lost your family, your job, your friends, your health. You may be sitting in a prison on death row, but you have not lost the Father's love!

The young man went to work for a local citizen, tending pigs. This was one of the most menial and despised jobs of the time. Applied spiritually, many people try to work their way out of their problems. You cannot go into the heavenly Father's presence based on your works.

The passage also says that no man helped him. Everyone had failed him. If everyone has failed you in your time of need, then you are in a good position to receive God's help because you are no longer looking to man expecting human assistance.

Eventually, the young man was filling his stomach with husks from the pig pen where he worked. The word *husks* actually refers to a long, hard, carob pod, with a tough and leathery shell. It grew on scrubby bushes and could not be consumed by humans. It was not really good for livestock either. There is no nourishment or nutrition in it.

Have you been trying to fill yourself with the empty husks and hard pods of this world? Fleshly, carnal living will always leave you hungry. You will starve feeding on the world's garbage of pornography, drugs, alcohol, and other empty things. Husks have no nutritional value, and they are not satisfying. There is a void in you that the husks of this world cannot fill.

What are you living on? Food from the Father's table or the swine's husks of the world?

HE CAME TO THE
END OF HIMSELF

Finally, this young man came to the end of himself. If that is where you are, then you are in a good position for a new beginning. As long as you are relying on friends, money, and your own resources, then you don't get this desperate. When all hope is gone (there is no one who can help, no friends, no money, nothing you can do to change your life), then these dire circumstances can be used of God to draw you back home to the Father.

You have a choice. You can remain where you are, hoping your friends will come through for you, remaining in the filth of the world and eating its empty husks, but a year from now you will be in the same pigpen. Same problems. Same emptiness.

This young man made a decision:

> *And when he came to himself, he said, How many hired servants of my father's have bread enough and to spare, and I perish with hunger!* (Luke 15:17)

Perish—that's the key word! This young man, who had deliberately walked away from God, was lonely, dissatisfied, lost, and perishing spiritually. Do you want to keep living life as you are now and perish, or do you want to do something to change your future?

When the young man came to himself, he remembered that in his father's house there was enough bread for everyone with plenty left over. There was bread enough to spare. No matter what you may need in order to begin again (forgiveness, deliverance, finances, healing), there is ample provision in the Father's house. Do not remain in the pigpen of life, perishing in the shadow of the promise of plenty.

The prodigal son's affliction caused reflection, which resulted in a change of direction:

> *I will arise and go to my father, and will say unto him, Father, I have sinned against heaven, and before thee, And am no*

more worthy to be called thy son: make me as one of thy hired servants (Luke 15:18-19).

There was no bargaining. He didn't think, *If he says this, then I will say that.* There were no terms for surrender. The young man took total responsibility for his own sin and dire circumstances.

The backslider must take words of repentance and return to the Father:

Take with you words, and turn to the Lord: say unto Him, Take away all iniquity, and receive us graciously: so will we render the calves of our lips (Hosea 14:2).

When this young man left the father's house, he was saying, "Give me, give me." When he returned, he was saying, "Make me!" He knew that he needed a total overhaul, a second chance, a new beginning.

This young man was only hoping to be a hired servant, which was the lowliest kind of laborer in that day. Regular servants lived in the house of their masters and had some rights and privileges. Hired servants were contracted on a daily basis to do the lowest, most menial tasks. That is all the repentant young man hoped for.

HE ACTED ON HIS DECISION

It is not enough to make a decision for a new start. You must act upon that decision. Faith is a fact, but it is also an act. You can decide that things need to change, but if you don't act on that decision, there will be no change.

Year after year, people make New Year's resolutions. They realize that they need a fresh start, and they decide to turn over a new leaf. They want to break with the past. For a time, they may do so, but it doesn't last. Gradually, they slide back into the old patterns of behavior. Finally, they come to the conclusion that it is hopeless.

When the prodigal son wanted a change in his life, he acted upon his decision, got up, and started on his journey home:

And he arose, and came to his father. But when he was yet a great way off, his father saw him, and had compassion, and ran, and fell on his neck, and kissed him (Luke 15:20).

Do you notice the pattern here? First there is rebellion. Then there is a realization of one's condition. Then comes repentance and returning to the Father's house. Then there is the compassionate reception and restoration.

If you have walked away from God, this is the same pattern you must follow for your fresh start. You must realize your condition, repent, return to and be received by the Father, and accept His restoration. The only way to have a real and enduring second chance and new beginning is to return to the Father. Don't make resolutions. Return for restoration.

While this young man was a great distance down the road, his father saw him, had compassion on him, and ran to meet him. This is the only time in Scripture we have an analogy of our heavenly Father running, and it is in welcoming response to a child who has deliberately walked away and wants to return home.

The word *compassion* means "to be touched by a person's need and to suffer with them." Our heavenly Father God sees your need and has compassion on your suffering. Your heavenly Father sees you, too. He was watching you in that far country. His compassion does not fail.

Despite the fact the young man was in rags and smelled like a pigpen, the father embraced him. You don't have to get cleaned up to come to Him. He is waiting for your return, just as you are.

There is no sin so great, no pit so deep that you cannot return home. The way back home is open to you by the blood of Jesus:

But now in Christ Jesus ye who sometimes were far off are made nigh by the blood of Christ. For He is our peace, who hath made both one, and hath broken down the middle wall of partition between us; Having abolished in His flesh the enmity, even the law of commandments contained in ordinances; for to make in Himself of twain one new man, so making peace; And that He might reconcile both unto God in one body by the cross, having slain the enmity thereby: And came and preached peace to you which were afar off, and to them that were nigh (Ephesians 2:13-17).

Because of the blood of Jesus, you can return to the Father's house. Every partition erected by your sin and rebellion can been broken down. There is reconciliation, peace, and forgiveness awaiting you when you return. A new life awaits!

THE SON SAID—THE FATHER SAID

And the son said unto him, Father, I have sinned against heaven, and in thy sight, and am no more worthy to be called thy son. But the father said to his servants, Bring forth the best robe, and put it on him; and put a ring on his hand, and shoes on his feet (Luke 15:21-22).

The prodigal son felt that he was no longer worthy to be a son. His father had a different opinion. You may view yourself as unworthy to return to the Father. The enemy may tell you that you are unworthy. God speaks a different opinion over your life. Who will you listen to? The voices of satan and self, or the voice of your Father?

The prodigal son's father stripped the rags of the far country off his son, which is representative of the old life. A similar scene is described by the prophet Zechariah:

And he answered and spake unto those that stood before him, saying, Take away the filthy garments from him. And unto him he said, Behold, I have caused thine iniquity to pass from thee, and I will clothe thee with change of raiment (Zechariah 3:4).

The father called for the best robe, which is representative of the new life. Did you notice that he called for the *best* robe? Just because you rebelled, walked away from God, and lived in the far country of sin for a time does not mean that you have to settle for second best when you return. God has the *best* plan for you. There is no second-rate plan. There are no second-hand clothes. There is no "Plan B." There is only the best! God's desire is:

> *...that ye put on the new man, which after God is created in righteousness and true holiness* (Ephesians 4:24).

The father gave his son his ring, which gave him authority as an heir. These rings were used to seal important documents in Bible times. When you return, God not only gives you the robe of righteousness for the rags of your sin, but he gives you His power and authority, signifying that you are His heir. You are a son.

The father calls for shoes for his son. In Bible days, servants went barefoot. Shoes were only worn by the sons:

> *And because ye are sons, God hath sent forth the Spirit of his Son into your hearts, crying, Abba, Father. Wherefore thou art no more a servant, but a son; and if a son, then an heir of God through Christ* (Galatians 4:6-7).

The father held a great feast for his returning son:

> *And bring hither the fatted calf, and kill it; and let us eat, and be merry: For this my son was dead, and is alive again; he was lost, and is found. And they began to be merry* (Luke 15:23-24).

"Bring the fatted calf," said the father. "I've been preparing it all this time for my son's return." God is just waiting to give you a second chance. He has good things prepared for you. Why not return to the Father's house today?

Did you notice in the story that the father called his servants to bring the robe, the shoes, and prepare the fatted calf? If you are already in the heavenly Father's house, then he wants to use you to cover the errant sinner with the robe of compassion. The heavenly Father wants to use you in the ministry of reconciliation to bring prodigals back into right relationship with Him:

And all things are of God, who hath reconciled us to himself by Jesus Christ, and hath given to us the ministry of reconciliation; To wit, that God was in Christ, reconciling the world unto himself, not imputing their trespasses unto them; and hath committed unto us the word of reconciliation (2 Corinthians 5:18-19).

THE SECOND SON

There is a second son in this story. He is the older son who remained with his father during the prodigal's absence:

Now his elder son was in the field: and as he came and drew nigh to the house, he heard musick and dancing. And he called one of the servants, and asked what these things meant. And he said unto him, Thy brother is come; and thy father hath killed the fatted calf, because he hath received him safe and sound. And he was angry, and would not go in: therefore came his father out, and intreated him. And he answering said to his father, Lo, these many years do I serve thee, neither transgressed I at any time thy commandment: and yet thou never gavest me a kid, that I might make merry with my friends: But as soon as this thy son was come, which hath devoured thy living with harlots, thou hast killed for him the fatted calf. And he said unto him, Son, thou art ever with me, and all that I have is thine. It was meet that we should make merry, and be glad: for this thy brother was dead, and is alive again; and was lost, and is found (Luke 15:25-32).

This is a sad footnote to the story of the prodigal son. It is the account of the older brother, who refused the father's invitation to come into the father's house and join the celebration. Two major barriers blocked his entrance, his unforgiveness and his lack of understanding.

Unforgiveness

The older son was indignant with his younger brother. He couldn't believe that one with such poor character and shady past should have a place in the Father's house! He wouldn't even call him *brother*. He referred to him as, "This, thy son."

Understanding

The older son was indignant with his father because he didn't understand his ways. His carnal understanding kept him outside the father's house. How could the father forgive such wasteful, degrading, sinful behavior?

This man remained in the field of religion and self-righteousness instead of the household of salvation. He said, "I served thee (religion). I never left you and sinned like he did (self-righteousness)." This young man felt that he could earn relationship and position in the father's house.

The older son was not shut out of the feast by the father, but he shut himself out through his lack of forgiveness and his lack of understanding. Unforgiveness and a failure to understand the ways of the heavenly Father block the doorway to a new beginning for many people. If you need to forgive, do it! If you don't understand God's ways, admit it, and then trust Him by faith.

The father came out and begged the older son to come inside, but he refused. By refusing, this young man missed the joy in the father's house. There was food, fellowship, friends, and fun. All that he needed, all that he desired, awaited him in the father's house. All that you have ever desired awaits you in the house of your heavenly Father.

We spoke of a pattern in this story: rebellion, realization of one's condition, repentance, and returning to the Father's house, the compassionate reception and restoration. Here we see a sad alternative to this divine pattern: refusal—refusal to respond to the Father's invitation.

The story ends here. It is unfinished and unresolved. Each person writes his or her own ending to the parable, depending on the person's response to the grace and love of God. Being true believers, we should embrace those who return to the Father, no matter how long their absence or how vile their sin.

My brother and sister, standing outside in the darkness, refusing to accept those to whom God is giving a second chance, there may be a great deal that you think justifies your attitude. The Father appeals to you, as He did to this elder son. Come in out of the cold. Share in the Father's compassion and grace. Embrace your errant returning brother or sister with God's love and forgiveness.

The door is open to you:

> *And the Spirit and the bride say, Come. And let him that heareth say, Come. And let him that is athirst come. And whosoever will, let him take the water of life freely* (Revelation 22:17).

THE THIRD SON

Do you know that there is another son in this parable? It is the Son of God who told the story. God loved us so much that He sent His Son to the far country of this sinful world to take us back to the Father's house, to give us a new life, and to give us a second chance.

Why not take hold of His extended hand right now? Rise up from the pigpen of your rebellion and sin, and return to the Father's house. He is waiting just for you. This time, you will not fail. You will be able to maintain your new life. You will learn how in the next chapter.

MAINTAINING YOUR NEW LIFE

When you began this journey to a new beginning, you learned that you must have a spiritual mind in order to receive your new life because *"...the natural man receiveth not the things of the Spirit of God: for they are foolishness unto him; neither can he know them, because they are spiritually discerned"* (1 Cor. 2:14). When you receive your new beginning, you must live it out in the Spirit just as you received it—through the Spirit.

It is one thing to obtain, another to maintain. For example, it is relatively easy to obtain a state of matrimony. Stand before a minister or judge, and repeat the vows. It is another thing to maintain the marriage over the course of years, in the midst of sickness, financial difficulties, disagreements, and other hardships.

That is why it is important that you not only obtain a new life, but you learn how to maintain it. In this chapter, you will learn how to maintain the new life God gives you.

WHAT IS THE KEY?

What is the key to living your new life? How can you be assured you will not fail? To discover the answer, let us go to the story of a man named Lazarus in John chapter 11:

Now a certain man was sick, named Lazarus, of Bethany, the town of Mary and her sister Martha. (It was that Mary which anointed the Lord with ointment, and wiped his feet with her hair, whose brother Lazarus was sick.) Therefore his sisters sent unto him, saying, Lord, behold, he whom thou lovest is sick. When Jesus heard that, he said, This sickness is not unto death, but for the glory of God, that the Son of God might be glorified thereby. Now Jesus loved Martha, and her sister, and Lazarus. When he had heard therefore that he was sick, he abode two days still in the same place where he was. ...Then when Jesus came, he found that he had lain in the grave four days already... (John 11:1-39).

When their brother took sick, Mary and Martha sent for Jesus immediately but He didn't come right away. By the time He arrived, Lazarus had been dead four days. These women had lost hope. They may have felt Jesus didn't really care because He didn't show up when they thought He should.

Have you ever felt that way? That Jesus wasn't really there when you needed Him? You had your idea of what He should do, but when it didn't work out that way you gave up hope. The Word declares:

For my thoughts are not your thoughts, neither are your ways my ways, saith the Lord. For as the heavens are higher than the earth, so are my ways higher than your ways, and my thoughts than your thoughts (Isaiah 55:8-9).

When God delays, it is because He has a greater plan and purpose. Jesus didn't come when Lazarus was sick, He waited until he was dead. Do you feel dead inside? Have you buried your dreams? Has your relationship with God and others died? Does it seem you have no future? That is exactly what the Master has been waiting for. He has been waiting for your realization that without His resurrection power, you cannot live a new life. When God delays, it is because He has a greater miracle, a greater purpose to accomplish in your life.

When Martha heard that Jesus had arrived, she rushed out to meet Him while her sister, Mary, waited in the house. Then said Martha unto Jesus: *"...Lord, if thou hadst been here, my brother had not died"* (John 11:21).

Have you uttered words like these? "Jesus, if you had been here, my dream would not have died." "My marriage would not have failed." "My finances would not have been lost." Note what Martha said next: *"But I know, that even now, whatsoever thou wilt ask of God, God will give it thee"* (John 11:22). Martha declared that even though her brother was dead, nothing was impossible to the Lord:

> *Jesus saith unto her, Thy brother shall rise again. Martha saith unto him, I know that he shall rise again in the resurrection at the last day. Jesus said unto her, I am the resurrection, and the life: he that believeth in Me, though he were dead, yet shall he live: And whosoever liveth and believeth in Me shall never die. Believest thou this? She saith unto Him, Yea, Lord: I believe that Thou art the Christ, the Son of God, which should come into the world* (John 11:23-27).

Jesus declared to Martha: *"...I am the resurrection, and the life: he that believeth in Me, though he were dead, yet shall he live"* (John 11:25).

There is no past day of miracles. God still heals and delivers. The Master is still miraculously restoring dead lives spiritually. *I am* is present tense. He is the *I am* in your life today, in any situation where you need the resurrecting power of God.

> *And when she had so said, she went her way, and called Mary her sister secretly, saying, The Master is come, and calleth for thee. As soon as she heard that, she arose quickly, and came unto Him. ...Then when Mary was come where Jesus was, and saw Him, she fell down at His feet, saying unto Him, Lord, if Thou hadst been here, my brother had not died* (John 11:28-32).

When Jesus saw the pain that Mary and Martha and their friends were experiencing, He *"...groaned in the spirit, and was troubled"* (John 11:33). Then, when He was led to Lazarus' grave site, *"Jesus wept"* (John 11:35).

Jesus was not only groaning and weeping for all those who would experience the devastating effects of physical death, but it is possible He was also weeping for those whose dreams had died, whose visions had been laid to rest, whose relationships had failed. Then Jesus said,

> *...Where have ye laid him? They said unto Him, Lord, come and see. Jesus wept. Then said the Jews, Behold how He loved him! And some of them said, Could not this Man, which opened the eyes of the blind, have caused that even this man should not have died? Jesus therefore again groaning in Himself cometh to the grave. It was a cave, and a stone lay upon it. Jesus said, Take ye away the stone. Martha, the sister of him that was dead, saith unto Him, Lord, by this time he stinketh: for he hath been dead four days. Jesus saith unto her, Said I not unto thee, that, if thou wouldest believe, thou shouldest see the glory of God? Then they took away the stone from the place where the dead was laid. And Jesus lifted up His eyes, and said, Father, I thank Thee that Thou hast heard Me. And I knew that Thou hearest Me always: but because of the people which stand by I said it, that they may believe that Thou hast sent Me. And when He thus had spoken, He cried with a loud voice, Lazarus, come forth. And he that was dead came forth, bound hand and foot with graveclothes: and his face was bound about with a napkin. Jesus saith unto them, Loose him, and let him go. Then many of the Jews which came to Mary, and had seen the things which Jesus did, believed on Him* (John 11:34-45).

When Jesus came on the scene and gave the command to come forth, death was swallowed up in victory! Lazarus came forth to new life in resurrection power. It is perhaps the greatest new beginning recorded in the Bible.

Where have you laid your dead dream? Let Jesus speak resurrection life back into it today. Speak to your dream yourself. Say, *"Dream, LIVE, in the name of Jesus!"*

RECEIVING RESURRECTION LIFE

The same power that raised Lazarus from the dead is the power that is at work in you. The Bible declares:

> *But if the Spirit of Him that raised up Jesus from the dead dwell in you, He that raised up Christ from the dead shall also quicken your mortal bodies by His Spirit that dwelleth in you* (Romans 8:11).

The same Spirit that raised Jesus Christ from the dead, the same spirit that raised Lazarus, dwells in you to quicken you right now! Paul continues:

> *Therefore, brethren, we are debtors, not to the flesh, to live after the flesh. For if ye live after the flesh, ye shall die: but if ye through the Spirit do mortify the deeds of the body, ye shall live. For as many as are led by the Spirit of God, they are the sons of God* (Romans 8:12-14).

These verses have often been used to emphasize the glorious resurrection that will take place when the physical body will be resurrected and we will exchange it for an immortal body. Praise God for this glorious reality! As you read the entire message of Romans chapter 8, you will see that Paul was writing to the Romans about walking in the Spirit versus walking in the flesh. Yes, there will be a resurrection of our body in the future, but there is also a glorious resurrection to life in the Spirit now.

The only way you can maintain your new life is through resurrection power—that same Spirit that raised Christ from the dead. That Spirit will keep you from living a fleshly life that results in death—death to dreams, relationships, your future. When you walk in the Spirit, you will not fail because you are being led and directed by the Spirit of God.

When you were born again, you were given new life spiritually. It was given to you by the Spirit that God placed within you—His own Spirit! You have been resurrected from the dead to become a temple of the Holy Spirit: *"...for ye are the temple of the living God; as God hath said, I will dwell in them, and walk in them; and I will be their God, and they shall be My people"* (2 Cor. 6:16).

Jesus walked in the full knowledge of God, knowing that the Father was in Him. In order for you to walk in the fullness of the Holy Spirit, you must also walk in the full knowledge of God. You must live every day of your life in the awareness that Christ is in you. You are dead, and He is living His life in you. That is truly new life!

You have been given a spiritual heart transplant. God has removed the stony heart that caused you to live in the flesh and He has given you a new heart with which to love, obey, and serve Him. You now owe a debt! *"... we are debtors, not to the flesh, to live after the flesh"* (Rom. 8:12). You are responsible to make sure that you no longer live your life walking after and gratifying your own flesh but that you live your life after the Spirit. It is not a matter of choice:

> *So, since Christ suffered in the flesh for us, for you, arm your-selves with the same thought and purpose [patiently to suffer rather than fail to please God]. For whoever has suffered in the flesh [having the mind of Christ] is done with [intentional] sin [has stopped pleasing himself and the world, and pleases God], So that he can no longer spend the rest of his natural life living by [his] human appetites and desires, but [he lives] for what God wills* (1 Peter 4:1-2 AMP).

The suffering in the flesh mentioned in this verse is not referring to the physical infirmities of pain, sickness, or disease. This suffering is referring to crucifying (putting to death) the fleshly desires and appetites of the body. Now that you have spiritually risen from the dead with Christ, you must set your mind, will, and emotions on the things of God.

If then you have been raised with Christ [to a new life, thus sharing His resurrection from the dead], aim at and seek the [rich, eternal treasures] that are above, where Christ is, seated at the right hand of God. [Ps. 110:1] And set your minds and keep them set on what is above (the higher things), not on the things that are on the earth. For [as far as this world is concerned] you have died, and your [new, real] life is hidden with Christ in God. When Christ, Who is our life, appears, then you also will appear with Him in [the splendor of His] glory. So kill (deaden, deprive of power) the evil desire lurking in your members [those animal impulses and all that is earthly in you that is employed in sin]: sexual vice, impurity, sensual appetites, unholy desires, and all greed and covetousness, for that is idolatry (the deifying of self and other created things instead of God) (Colossians 3:1-5 AMP).

YIELDING TO THE SPIRIT

Not only are you given new life by the Spirit that lives within you, but you are brought into a greater knowledge of Christ. Jesus told His disciples that the Comforter (Holy Spirit) would not speak for Himself but would testify about Jesus to them. (Read John 15:26 and 16:13.)

Your experience is limited to the degree of your grasp of God's purpose and plan for your life. Let that statement sink down deep into your spirit. Think about it. When you were first born again, you were a newborn baby spiritually. You had a limited understanding of God's purpose for your life. More than likely, you didn't fully understand what had happened to you.

Then, as you began to read and study God's Word, His Spirit began to remove the veil of darkness and unfold His plan and purpose for your life. The Spirit began to teach and guide you into all truth. It was not until you began to grasp these promises and act on them in faith that you were brought into an experience of possessing and enjoying them.

This is your time for a new beginning. As the Holy Spirit reveals to you the new plans He has for you, receive this revelation in faith and begin to act on it to make it a reality in your life.

The work of the Holy Spirit is not automatic. You must continually yield to the Spirit. As long as you continue to release your faith and act on the truths that the Spirit reveals, you will continue to grow, mature, and embrace the new things of God.

You have been born again by the Spirit. God has placed His resurrecting Spirit within you. He dwells in you. By that same Spirit, He is revealing His plan and purpose for your life:

> *But we all, with open face beholding as in a glass the glory of the Lord, are changed into the same image from glory to glory, even as by the Spirit of the Lord* (2 Corinthians 3:18).

God wants you to come into an experience where you have been baptized—totally immersed—in the Holy Spirit. He has planned for you to face the enemy in the fullness of the Holy Spirit, as Jesus did. He has planned that the same *dunamis* power of the Holy Spirit that was manifested in Jesus' life will be manifested in your life.

REMAINING FULL OF THE SPIRIT

To remain full of the Holy Spirit you must continually come to the source of the life-giving stream. Jesus is the Source:

> *Now on the final and most important day of the Feast, Jesus stood, and He cried in a loud voice, If any man is thirsty, let him come to Me and drink! He who believes in Me [who cleaves to and trusts in and relies on Me] as the Scripture has said, From his innermost being shall flow [continuously] springs and rivers of living water. But He was speaking here of the Spirit, Whom those who believed (trusted, had faith) in Him were afterward to receive. For the [Holy] Spirit had not*

yet been given, because Jesus was not yet glorified (raised to honor) (John 7:37-39 AMP).

On this occasion, Jesus made one of the most earthshaking announcements of His entire ministry. This was not a spontaneous incident in His life. He chose this particular time—during the Feast of Tabernacles—to publicly proclaim Himself to be the Messiah, the Anointed One, the Baptizer in the Holy Spirit.

At this particular time, Jesus was facing growing persecution from the Pharisees. They hated Him and were seeking every opportunity to kill him. Because of the opposition, Jesus had not gone to Judea to minister among the Jewish people. He remained in Galilee, teaching and ministering there.

He was also facing opposition from His own family. Even Jesus' brothers did not believe in Him. They did not recognize Him to be the promised Messiah. As they were preparing to go to Jerusalem to observe the Feast of Tabernacles, they told Jesus:

> *His brethren therefore said unto Him, Depart hence, and go into Judaea, that Thy disciples also may see the works that Thou doest. For there is no man that doeth any thing in secret, and he himself seeketh to be known openly. If Thou do these things, shew Thyself to the world. For neither did His brethren believe in Him* (John 7:3-5).

Jesus was not afraid to go to Judea. He knew God's plan and purpose for His life. He knew God was in control of the circumstances that He faced. He told them: *"Go ye up unto this feast: I got not up yet unto this feast; for My time is not yet full come. When He had said these words unto them, He abode still in Galilee"* (John 7:8-9).

After His brothers left to go to the feast, Jesus secretly went to Jerusalem. Instead of traveling with a large caravan, He traveled alone. He wasn't afraid. He knew the importance of spiritual timing. He was walking in the fullness of the Spirit.

In the middle of the feast, Jesus suddenly appeared in the Temple and began teaching. As He taught, there was a great division among the people.

Some believed that Jesus was the Messiah. Others thought that He was an imposter. There were also those who were undecided.

As Jesus taught openly in the Temple, the people murmured and whispered among themselves:

> ...Isn't this the Man they are trying to kill? Here He is, speaking publicly, and they are not saying a word to Him. Have the authorities really concluded that He is the Christ? But we know where this Man is from; when the Christ comes, no one will know where He is from (John 7:25-27 NIV).

Fearlessly, and with great power and authority, Jesus cried out with a loud voice:

> ...Yes, you know Me, and you know where I am from. I am not here on My own, but He who sent Me is true. You do not know Him, but I know Him because I am from Him and He sent me (John 7:28-29 NIV).

Jesus openly proclaimed that He was the Messiah, the One who was sent from God.

Then came that last great day of the feast. On this special day, the people gathered together to commemorate God's supernatural provision during the time that Israel traveled through the desert with Moses. One such provision was when the rock poured forth water for them to drink, a symbolic example of the promised outpouring of the Holy Spirit. (Read Joel 2:28.)

A solemn procession—headed by a priest carrying a golden pitcher—gathered water from the pool of Siloam. When they returned to the Temple, the people watched the priest pour the water out on the west side of the altar. Imagine that you were there at that strategic moment, seeing the beautiful, golden pitcher glistening in the sun, with all eyes focused upon the water that was slowly being poured out.

Suddenly, seemingly from out of nowhere, a loud cry could be heard. Heads and eyes turned toward the direction of the voice. There, standing in a prominent place, was Jesus. With great power and authority, He declared:

> ...*If any man thirst, let him come unto Me, and drink. He that believeth on Me, as the scripture hath said, out of his belly shall flow rivers of living water* (John 7:37-38).

Jesus was declaring that He was the rock who would be smitten for their sins. He was the Water of life who would be poured out for them. If they were spiritually thirsty and seeking the living God, they could come to Him and drink.

Jesus was not talking about giving them a drink of water. He was talking about the Holy Spirit: *"(But this spake He of the Spirit, which they that believe on Him should receive: for the Holy Ghost was not yet given; because that Jesus was not yet glorified)"* (John 7:39).

Do you remember how you felt before you were born again? Then, when you came to Jesus, you received a drink of the life-giving Spirit of the living God and He gave you His Spirit to dwell within you. You received life. Your thirst was quenched.

In these verses, Jesus was not only referring to the new life that you received when you were born again. He did not just offer a single one-time drink of water. He said that the water would be overflowing. He didn't say that there would be a little trickle of water. He said that out of your innermost being would flow rivers of living water—rivers of the Holy Spirit—to meet the needs of those around you.

In the natural world, how long do you think you could go without having a drink of water? An average human being—doing light work in a temperate climate—loses nearly five pints of water a day. Just breathing, man uses nearly one pint of water daily. According to medical findings, in a matter of days without water, the tissues in the body will begin to deteriorate and eventually a person will die. Man cannot survive without water. To remain healthy and strong, you must have a steady intake of water.

ALL TRUTH IS PARALLEL

All truth is parallel. In the spiritual world, you must have a continual flow of the new water of life of the Holy Spirit. Without a continual intake of the life-giving Spirit, you will spiritually dry up and die. You must continue to come to Him and drink until you are totally immersed in, possessed by, and controlled by the Holy Spirit.

There is no other way to remain full of the Holy Spirit but to continually come to drink of the Spirit. As you come, you are not coming to receive salvation again. You are coming to drink, to receive a fresh intake of the Spirit.

As you keep coming and keep drinking, the fire of the Holy Spirit will continue to purge out the sinful desires in your life. The *dunamis,* miracle-working power of God, will flow in a continual stream through your life. You will continually be changing into Christ's image. You will be continually filled—full, to overflowing—with the Holy Spirit. You will walk in the fullness of the Holy Spirit and continually embrace new things in God.

Are you spiritually thirsty? Is there a hungering and thirsting deep within your spirit for God to totally possess your being? Do you want to be baptized—full of and controlled by—the Holy Spirit? Don't seek the prayer language of other tongues. Don't seek the outward signs. These are only manifestations of the Spirit. The power and the gifts will come as you allow the Holy Spirit to flow through you. Seek the source of the living water, Jesus Christ!

One reason so many Christians are defeated is that they are trying to face their circumstances in their own strength. There are preachers, teachers, evangelists, singers, and other Christian workers who are trying to spiritually conquer and tear down satan's strongholds in their own strength. How did the Church get into the position of being more dependent on its own abilities, its man-made programs, and man-made formulas for success than on the power and anointing of the Holy Spirit?

It is the anointing of the Holy Spirit that breaks every yoke of bondage. It is the anointing of the Holy Spirit that enables you to have a new beginning. It will take the anointing of the Holy Spirit to make you victorious in the day-to-day circumstances that you face and help you successfully maintain your new life.

As you enter into the new things God has for you, defeat will not be an option because you will be walking in the fullness of the Holy Spirit. God has not planned any defeats for you. He has planned victory for you in every area of your life as you learn to live daily in the resurrection power of the Holy Spirit.

You are assured of maintaining your new beginning because that same Spirit that raised Christ from the dead dwells in you! It is the resurrecting power of Almighty God, and (as you will learn in the next chapter) it will continually manifest new things in your life.

CHAPTER 15

BEHOLD, I MAKE ALL THINGS NEW

The Bible begins with God creating new things—the entire world and all that is therein. The Bible ends with God still creating new things—a new Heaven and a new earth. In between the Books of Genesis and Revelation, He continually does new things.

Although this is the last chapter of this book, in reality your spiritual journey to a new life does not end here. You will constantly experience new beginnings as God continues to do new things in your life. Paul declared:

> *For we know that our old self was crucified with Him so that the body of sin might be done away with, that we should no longer be slaves to sin—because anyone who has died has been freed from sin. Now if we died with Christ, we believe that we will also live with Him* (Romans 6:6-8 NIV).

You were freed from sin, resurrected from the old life, and baptized into Christ for the purpose of living a new life!

THE NEW THINGS OF GOD

God has declared:

Remember ye not the former things, neither consider the things of old. Behold, I will do a new thing; now it shall spring forth; shall ye not know it? I will even make a way in the wilderness, and rivers in the desert (Isaiah 43:18-19).

Our Creator is constantly doing new things. Here are a few of the new things He has promised in His Word:

He established a new covenant with you through the blood of Jesus:

In that He saith, A new covenant, He hath made the first old. Now that which decayeth and waxeth old is ready to vanish away (Hebrews 8:13).

…This cup is the New Testament of My blood which is shed for you (Luke 22:20).

He makes you a new creature in Christ:

Therefore if any man be in Christ, he is a new creature: old things are passed away; behold, all things are become new (2 Corinthians 5:17).

He has made a new way for you to enter into His presence:

Having therefore, brethren, boldness to enter into the holiest by the blood of Jesus. By a new and living way which He hath consecrated for us, through the vail, that is to say, His flesh (Hebrews 10:19-20).

He gives you a new spirit and a new heart:

And I will give them one heart, and I will put a new spirit within you; and I will take the stony heart out of their flesh and will give them an heart of flesh; That they may walk in

My statutes and keep Mine ordinances, and do them; and they shall be My people, and I will be their God (Ezekiel 11:19-20).

A new heart also will I give you, and a new spirit will I put within you; and I will take away the stony heart out of your flesh, and I will give you an heart of flesh. And I will put My spirit within you... (Ezekiel 36:26-27).

He gives you a new mind:

Let this mind be in you which was also in Christ Jesus (Philippians 2:5).

He gives you new thoughts:

For My thoughts are not your thoughts, neither are your ways My ways, saith the Lord. For as the heavens are higher than the earth, so are My ways higher than your ways, and My thoughts than your thoughts (Isaiah 55:8-9).

He makes your latter years greater than the former:

The glory of this latter house shall be greater than the former, saith the Lord of hosts... (Haggai 2:9).

He gives you a new song:

Sing unto Him a new song; play skillfully with a loud noise (Psalm 33:3).

He gives you new tongues and spiritual revelations:

And it shall come to pass afterward, that I will pour out My spirit upon all flesh; and your sons and your daughters shall prophesy, and your old men shall dream dreams, your young men shall see visions. And also upon the servants and upon the hand-maids in those days will I pour out My spirit (Joel 2:28-29).

He extends new mercies daily to you:

This I recall to mind, therefore have I hope. It is of the Lord's mercies that we are not consumed, because his compassions fail not. They are new every morning; great is thy faithfulness (Lamentations 3:21-23).

NEW VESSELS FOR NEW WINE

God promised: *"Behold, the former things are come to pass, and new things do I declare: before they spring forth I tell you of them"* (Isa. 42:9). The things of the past are the former things. God wants you to be a vessel ready to receive the new things He has prepared for you:

But as it is written, Eye hath not seen, nor ear heard, neither have entered into the heart of man, the things which God hath prepared for them that love Him. But God hath revealed them unto us by His Spirit: for the Spirit searcheth all things, yea, the deep things of God. For what man knoweth the things of a man, save the spirit of man which is in him? even so the things of God knoweth no man, but the Spirit of God. Now we have received, not the spirit of the world, but the spirit which is of God; that we might know the things that are freely given to us of God (1 Corinthians 2:9-12).

God will continue to reveal new things to you by His Spirit, but you must be ready to receive them. Jesus addressed this issue in two short illustrations:

No man putteth a piece of new cloth unto an old garment, for that which is put in to fill it up taketh from the garment, and the rent is made worse. Neither do men put new wine into old bottles: else the bottles break, and the wine runneth out, and the bottles perish: but they put new wine into new bottles, and both are preserved (Matthew 9:16-17).

If you patch an old garment, the garment may shrink and pull the patch loose. God doesn't want a patched up version of what you were. He doesn't want to patch up the old—He wants to create the new.

In Bible days, wine was stored in wineskins made from the skins of sheep and goats. The new skins were flexible and would expand during the fermentation process. The old skins lost their elasticity and if you put new wine in them they would burst as the wine fermented.

You cannot contain the new things God wants to do in and through you in the old wineskins of traditions of the past. You must be like a new wineskin, flexible and continually open to new things and a fresh move of His Spirit.

WALKING IN THE SUPERNATURAL

There are six major obstacles you must guard against if you are to continue to embrace the new things of God and walk in the supernatural. These are drawn from the story of Peter's walk on the water:

Immediately Jesus made His disciples get into the boat and go before Him to the other side, while He sent the multitudes away. And when He had sent the multitudes away, He went up on the mountain by Himself to pray. Now when evening came, He was alone there. But the boat was now in the middle of the sea, tossed by the waves, for the wind was contrary. Now in the fourth watch of the night Jesus went to them, walking on the sea. And when the disciples saw Him walking on the sea, they were troubled, saying, "It is a ghost!" And they cried out for fear. But immediately Jesus spoke to them, saying, "Be of good cheer! It is I; do not be afraid." And Peter answered Him and said, "Lord, if it is You, command me to come to You on the water." So He said, "Come." And when Peter had come down out of the boat, he walked on the water to go to Jesus. But when he saw that the wind was boisterous, he was afraid; and beginning to sink he cried out, saying, "Lord, save me!" And immediately Jesus stretched out His hand and caught him, and said to him, "O you of little faith, why did you doubt?" And when they got into the boat, the wind ceased. Then those who were in the boat came and worshiped Him, saying, "Truly You are the Son of God" (Matthew 14:22-33 NKJV).

Jesus commanded His disciples to get into the boat and go before Him to the other side of the lake. We have been commanded to go into the world before Jesus, preparing the way for His return:

And this gospel of the kingdom will be preached in all the world as a witness to all the nations, and then the end will come (Matthew 24:14).

The disciples had a destiny: The other side. They had a purpose: Go before Me. You, too, have a destiny and purpose. When you are on the way to your destiny, to fulfill your divine purpose, you encounter the storms of life. How you respond to these storms will determine whether you continue to walk in the supernatural dimension of your new life.

Here are six major obstacles that you must guard against if you are to continue to walk in the supernatural and embrace the new things of God.

1. Familiarity

This is relying on what you know to do. Several of the disciples were fishermen. When they encountered the storm, they could have relied upon their own abilities. I am a fisherman. I know what to do. If I just change my sails; if I just alter the course of the boat a bit.

If you rely on what you know, you will be limited by your own abilities. You need supernatural resources in order to live your new life and accomplish your destiny. You can't calm the storm. You can't walk on water in your own strength. There is no handbook for some of the new things you will be called on to do. There is no guidebook titled *Three Steps to Walking on Water*.

2. *Fear*

The disciples were fearful when the storm struck, and all but Peter were afraid to get out of the boat at Christ's command. Fear will keep you from embracing new things. What would you attempt to do for God if you weren't afraid of failure?

3. *Friends*

Peter's friends remained in the boat. Don't let others tell you what to do or what can and can't be done. Don't follow their advice or their example. Like these disciples, even good Christian friends can be limited in their revelation. The other disciples saw Jesus, they finally recognized Him, but they didn't have the courage to go to Him.

4. *Faith*

In the strength of that one word, *Come*, Peter stepped out of the boat. If you are to reach your destiny, you must walk by faith, not by sight. When Jesus challenges you to embrace the new, be ready to step out of the boat of familiarity, tradition, etc., and respond.

5. *Focus*

As long as Peter kept his eyes on Jesus, he walked on the water—something new that had never been done by man. It was when Peter looked around at the swirling tempest that he began to sink. If you are to continue on in the new things of God, your focus must be kept on Jesus. Keep your eyes off the circumstances. Don't let the storm seize your attention and distract you from your destiny.

6. *Failure*

Peter failed when he looked around at the circumstances in the natural world and he began to sink. He failed in the natural, but learned a great lesson in the supernatural. Peter learned that he could not fulfill his destiny in himself. He cried out to Jesus, *"Depart from me, I am a sinful man."*

Peter would fail again when he denied Christ three times during the events preceding the Crucifixion. Again, Jesus would forgive him and give him a new beginning as a key leader in the first church.

Through these failures, Peter learned that obstacles were actually opportunities for the demonstration of God's power. That is why some time later Peter could say to a lame man at the temple gate, "In the name of Jesus, rise up and walk!" Peter learned from failure that there was only one way to walk in this new life—in the supernatural. When you learn to walk in the supernatural, you will be able to reach out to those in need and empower them to do the same.

Accept the challenge today. Get out of the boat of safety, tradition, and familiarity. Step into your new life. Embrace your destiny. Put a demand on your potential. Peter didn't know he could walk on water until he tried. This is your season for change. God will use you to pioneer uncharted territories in the spiritual world. He is launching you into a new dimension.

God has given you a new beginning not just to bless you, although He wants very much to do that. He has given you a new beginning for a divine purpose. There are fearful people caught in the storms of life who will only come to recognize Jesus if you step out of the boat and move toward your destiny.

There are lame men (spiritually, physically, emotionally, mentally) whose only hope is in a supernatural touch from one who has learned to walk in the supernatural, from one who has experienced a new beginning.

That is you!

Your new beginning is for divine purpose and destiny. Step out of the boat, and—through the supernatural power of God—walk into your new life.

Author Contact Information

Morris Cerullo World Evangelism
P.O. Box 85277
San Diego, CA 92186
858-277-2200

Morris Cerullo World Evangelism of Canada
P.O. Box 3600
Concord, Ontario L4K 1B6
905-669-1788

Morris Cerullo World Evangelism of Great Britain
P.O. Box 277
Hemel Hempstead, Herts HP2 7DH
(0) 1442-232432

Web site: www.mcwe.com
E-mail: morriscerullo@mcwe.com

Additional copies of this book and other
book titles from DESTINY IMAGE are
available at your local bookstore.

Call toll-free: 1-800-722-6774.

Send a request for a catalog to:

Destiny Image® Publishers, Inc.

P.O. Box 310
Shippensburg, PA 17257-0310

*"Speaking to the Purposes of God for This
Generation and for the Generations to Come."*

**For a complete list of our titles,
visit us at www.destinyimage.com.**